SHEEP

SUNRISE ON THE RANGE

SHEEP
Life on the South Dakota Range

ARCHER B. GILFILLAN

With a New Introduction by
Richard W. Etulain

Illustrations by Kurt Wiese

MINNESOTA HISTORICAL SOCIETY PRESS
St. Paul

Cover: Archer B. Gilfillan's sheep wagon, Friends of the Middle Border Museum, Mitchell, South Dakota; photograph courtesy of Jennewein Collections, Layne Library, Dakota Wesleyan University, Mitchell.

Borealis Books are high-quality paperback reprints of books chosen by the Minnesota Historical Society Press for their importance as enduring historical sources and their value as enjoyable accounts of life in the Upper Midwest.

♾ The paper used in this publication meets the minimum requirements of the American National Standard for Information Sciences — Permanence for Printed Library Materials, ANSI Z39.48–1984.

An earlier version of the "Introduction to the Reprint Edition" by Richard W. Etulain appeared as "Archer B. Gilfillan: Scholarly Sheepherder of South Dakota," *South Dakota History* 16 (Winter 1986): 373–91, and is used with the permission of the South Dakota State Historical Society.

Minnesota Historical Society Press, St. Paul 55102
First published 1929 by Little, Brown, and Company

International Standard Book Number 0–87351–285–5
Manufactured in the United States of America
10 9 8 7 6 5 4 3 2 1

Library of Congress Cataloging-in-Publication Data

Gilfillan, Archer B., b. 1886.
    Sheep : life on the South Dakota range / Archer B. Gilfillan ; with a new introduction by Richard W. Etulain ; illustrations by Kurt Wiese.
        p. cm. — (Borealis books)
    Originally published: Boston : Little, Brown, 1929.
    ISBN 0–87351–285–5 (alk. paper)
    1. Gilfillan, Archer B., b. 1886. 2. Shepherds—South Dakota—Harding County—Biography. 3. Sheep—South Dakota—Harding County. 4. Harding County (S.D.)—History. I. Title.
SF375.32.G55A3 1993
636.3'0092—dc20
[B]   92–42162

To
the best of sisters
EMILY MURIEL DEAN
this volume is affectionately dedicated

CONTENTS

	Introduction to the Reprint Edition	ix
	Preface	xxxv
	Prologue	xxxvii
I	Herding and Herders	3
II	Sheep Country	11
III	The Sheep Wagon	21
IV	The Herder's Partners	43
V	The Yearly Round	60
VI	Blast and Blizzard	83
VII	The Boss	93
VIII	Lambing and Shearing	102
IX	Sheep and Herder Traits	139
X	The Herder's Neighbors	159
XI	Reading and Other Amusements	197
XII	Hazards	216
XIII	Sheep Herder and Cowboy	230
XIV	Homesteads	244
XV	This Is the Life!	255

INTRODUCTION TO THE
REPRINT EDITION

ARCHER B. GILFILLAN was an anomaly. A Phi Beta
Kappa with a broad knowledge of classical literature and
language, a man with a nearly completed divinity degree, and a well-read person with a talent for writing, he
nonetheless turned his back on these attainments and
abilities to herd sheep for nearly twenty years in a lonely,
isolated part of the West. On the other hand, this
strange juxtaposition of an Ivy League education with almost two decades of sheepherding was undoubtedly the
major reason that Gilfillan produced the classic narrative
of American sheepherding. More than any other work,
Sheep provides a personal, informative, and entertaining account of the herder in the American West.[1]

By all accounts, Gilfillan became a sheepherder
through an unusual sequence of events. Born February 25, 1886, in White Earth, Minnesota, Archer was the
son of an Episcopal missionary to the Ojibway Indians
and grew up in a sheltered, highly religious, Victorian
home. His father suffered a nervous and physical break-
down from overwork when Archie was twelve, and the
family moved to Washington, D.C., where the children
attended church-related and public schools. But during
the summers Archie became intrigued with farming,
spending his vacations working on farms in Virginia,

Massachusetts, and Pennsylvania. Later, because of ill health and a trip to Europe with two of his aunts, he fell behind two years in school and did not enter high school until the fall of 1902 when he was sixteen. Short in stature and forced to wear glasses as the result of a serious bout with typhoid fever, Archie was sensitive about his size and thought others considered him a "sissy" because he did not participate in sports.[2]

But he did very well academically. A straight A student, a debater, and one who excelled in nearly all his courses, Archie graduated from high school in the spring of 1906 and entered Amherst College in the fall. When his younger brother spoke enthusiastically of his academic work at the University of Pennsylvania in Philadelphia, Archie decided to transfer to that institution, from which he graduated Phi Beta Kappa in 1910 with a special emphasis in Latin and Greek. As his younger sister has written, "for several years he had dreams of going west to make his fortune,"[3] so after graduating he escaped to South Dakota to begin work on a cattle ranch near the Black Hills.

Working for someone else did not fulfill his dreams, however, especially when, as he wrote later, he "contracted a severe case of land fever."[4] Asking for his share of the family estate — his father had inherited about two hundred thousand dollars from a wealthy relative — Archie homesteaded a section of land, built a cabin, and bought a small band of sheep and several horses. Ill at ease among hard-bargaining ranchers, he too often bought high and sold low. As a result, at the end of three years he had squandered a large portion of his legacy, which may have initially amounted to nearly ten thousand dollars.

His dreams turned to nightmares, and realizing his inabilities to handle his homestead and livestock, Gilfillan retreated to another possible occupation. Thinking he might have a call to the ministry, he entered Western Theological Seminary in Chicago, an Episcopal institution. He stayed for nearly three years but withdrew shortly before ordination ceremonies and joined the Roman Catholic church.

Archie was in a fix. Having lost perhaps more than half of his inheritance in his unsuccessful ranching venture and now alienated from the ministry, he fled west once again — this time to herd sheep in Harding County in the northwestern part of South Dakota. In 1916 he took the first job offered him as a herder on Alman H. Dean's AD ranch near Buffalo. Although he planned to stay only one year, while he decided his future, the months stretched into sixteen years.

These transitions were much more traumatic than Gilfillan admitted publicly. Indeed, the short space between 1929 and 1933 represented his swift rise and fall. If the publication of *Sheep* in 1929 symbolized the apex of his achievement, he was at his nadir four years later. Finding that the modest royalties from his book did not free him from herding and his mounting debts, unable to break the cycle of loneliness, insecurity, and alcoholism that bound him, and descending to new depths of despair after being badly beaten in an election for county treasurer in Harding County, Archer recorded the accumulating effect of these disappointments in his secret diary on May 3, 1932:

My whole life seemed to be in ruins. I had been almost sure for the past two years of winning office and
living in Buffalo. The defeat was apparently so crush-
ing that it not only killed my political hopes for the
present but for any time in the future.

Three months later Gilfillan was slipping fast. At-
tempting to find solace in alcohol, he plunged into a
feverish round of drinking that led to his eventual firing
after he was found drunk in his sheep wagon. As he admitted in his diary entry of August 11: "I hate to record
this day's doings worse than any that have gone into this
diary in seven years." And, the following December,
Archer summed up his lowest point: "I am lower in
worldly position than I have been yet. My book sale has
practically ended, I am dead politically, I have lost my
sixteen year long job, and I am discredited in my chosen
occupation."[5]

Setting up a small, rustic cabin along a creek in
Spearfish, Archer tried to regain his health and began
writing columns for several South Dakota newspapers.
Then a job as assistant state director of the New Deal-
sponsored writers' project in South Dakota opened in
Pierre, a position he held until the project ceased in the
spring of 1942. Through a friend he landed other employment at the Black Hills Ordnance Depot at Provo
(later renamed Igloo) where he did clerical work, wrote
for the *Igloo Magazine,* and served as librarian during his
seven-year stint. When his position at the depot ended
in 1949, he decided to move to Deadwood, where he
lived in retirement and declining health until his death
in 1955.

DURING HIS MANY YEARS on the range, Gilfillan did much more than herd sheep. A voracious reader, he followed a fairly well-organized reading program that included many volumes of ancient Greek, Roman, and English literature. Indeed, in one two-year period he waded through the fifty-volume Harvard Classics series, in addition to an "extensive list of books which he borrowed through the Alumni Extension Department of the University [of Pennsylvania] Library." He was particularly drawn to the writings of diarist Samuel Pepys and the works of various English dramatists. Writing to his alma mater, he told school officials that his career choice might not interest most of its students, but at least he could be held up "as a horrible example of a Phi Beta Kappa gone wrong, as a warning to future graduates."[6]

Gilfillan also turned to writing to fill his long days and nights on the range and in his sheep wagon. Initially he wrote local color sketches for the travel magazine *See America First,* but then he placed "The Sheep Herder" in the lordly *Saturday Evening Post,* which paid him seventy-five dollars for the lively essay.[7] Late in 1924, the same year as his appearance in the *Post,* he began a secret cipher diary. In the first entry of December 2, he confided: "I shall put down exactly what I think and do, without fear of its being read and consequently with all the honesty of which I am capable." For the next eight years and four months he recorded daily observations, totaling 9,010 pages in twenty-five bound volumes.[8] His close attention to detail, his growing knowledge and understanding of sheep and herding, his witty observations on the foibles of humans—all made for revealing entries. In addition, the diary discloses Gilfillan's persisting insecurities and isolation, his continuing troubled thoughts about women and his unfulfilled sexual desires, his mounting alcoholism, and his inabilities to break out of debt and find satisfying employment.

In 1928 and 1929 three sections of a book-length manuscript he called "Ten Years in a Sheep Wagon" (retitled *Sheep*) were published in the prestigious *Atlantic Monthly*. Editors at Little, Brown and Company, the book-publishing arm of *Atlantic,* first rejected the manuscript, but, Gilfillan recalled, "they couldn't get it out of their minds, and decided they would publish it as a book."[9] Gilfillan was ecstatic.

Although *Sheep* sold moderately well and was reprinted in the 1930s, Gilfillan did not immediately follow that sprightly written volume with other essays or plans for a second book. In 1933, however, his herding days over, he turned once again to his writing. During the next decade or so he contributed dozens of columns to South Dakota newspapers, commenting on local events and persons and providing general human-interest stories. In 1936 Gilfillan published the first of two collections of his latest essays. *A Shepherd's Holiday* gathered fifty-two selections about his life as a herder and his reflections on society and culture in South Dakota. After he had fully retired in the late 1940s, Gilfillan won a Regional Writing Fellowship of fifteen hundred dollars from the University of Minnesota, and during 1950–51 he gathered and rewrote some of his earlier columns, hoping that the University of Minnesota Press would publish them as a book. When the press rejected the collection, he tried other publishers, but none offered to publish his essays. Finally, a gathering was privately printed in 1953 as *A Goat's Eye View of the Black Hills.*[10]

Neither of these later books is as lengthy or as coherently organized as *Sheep*. If the chapters of *Sheep* center on Gilfillan's experience as a herder, the later collections are discursive, including additional considerations of herding, treatments of life and laughter in small-town South Dakota, and discussions of human foibles, local to universal. Even though the author treats broader sociocultural themes in these later anthologies than he did in *Sheep*, he is unable to focus his thoughts. One suspects that Gilfillan's tendency to scatter his ideas across expansive intellectual terrain was the major reason the essays were not commercially published. Moreover, *Sheep* had skimmed the cream from his rangeland experiences, leaving less solid and entertaining fare in the later collections.

Although not all responses to *Sheep* were entirely positive, most reviewers hailed it as the definitive study of sheepherding in the United States. The unnamed reviewer in the *New York Times* thought the book revealed a good deal about herding and promised readers they would "have many a hearty chuckle and many an explosive laugh over the author's dry humor." Another commentator pointed out that the book was "written with dry humor, keen observation and real love of the sheep." Still another reviewer called it a "surprisingly diverting document" in which the "narrative imparts the real flavor of life on the plains."[11]

IN WRITING *Sheep*, Gilfillan faced the difficulty of enlightening readers about an occupation not widely un-

derstood in the United States and one to which most
Americans attached little value. Sheepherders were the
lowest of the lowly in a cowboy culture. To face this
problem and to answer the question " 'Why is a sheep
herder, and How,' " (*Sheep,* xxxv) Gilfillan uses just the
right approach: a series of humorous anecdotal chapters,
laced with witty turns of phrase and told in a low-key ex-
positional style. In all, *Sheep* treats details of the herder's
daily life, comments upon several other topics, and
along the way reveals a good deal about the 1920s and
the personal opinions of its creator.

As one might expect, Gilfillan has much to say about
his rangeland competitor, the cowboy. Realizing that
the Stetsoned and booted cowpuncher outranks the
sheepherder in popular mythology like a purebred over
a mongrel, Gilfillan asks why this should be. The herder,
he argues, makes more money, he works longer hours,
and he carries more responsibility; yet the public cham-
pions the cowboy and forgets or ribs the sheepherder.
Throughout *Sheep* Gilfillan undercuts the man on
horseback and paints, in contrast, an appealing and interesting series of word pictures of herders and the matters of their daily lives.

Closely associated with Gilfillan's negative reactions to
exaggerated images of cowboys are his reservations about
a legendary Wild West. Repeatedly demythologizing
larger-than-life cowpunchers, he suggests that most
western rural workers experienced a mild, humdrum
West rather than a wild, adventurous one. In later essays, Gilfillan expands his comments to cover a popular,
tightly held mythic West. In two brief sketches entitled
"The Hero of the Westerns" and "The Cowboy of the

Pulps," he criticizes the widespread acceptance of heroic
fictional and cinematic cowboys in the popular culture of
the 1920s. After commenting on the stereotyped plots
and formulaic characters of westerns, Gilfillan concludes
that these yarns and characters have little place in "this
workaday world" that he and others inhabit. Even worse
are the pulp magazines of the 1930s, which, along with
other mediums, probably publish "more rot, drivel,
mawkish sentimentality and maudlin slush . . . about
the cowboy profession than any other half dozen call-
ings."[12] Gilfillan is convinced that these popular images
of the cowboy and Wild West not only do violence to the
truth but also displace the true workers of the West, including, of course, the sheepherder.

Later Gilfillan uses the figure of Calamity Jane to illustrate what he considers the negative impact of those
popular western images. Comparing the known facts
about Calamity's life with those presented in "her official
biography," in Hollywood extravaganzas, and in the
works of popular historians, Gilfillan asserts, is to con-
front a "wider divergence than is known in the case of
any comparable historical character." Although many
writers and films have depicted Calamity as beautiful,
feminine, and virginal, contemporary legal documents,
photographs, and newspapers portrayed a far different
picture.[13] In making this general argument and in select-
ing Calamity Jane as an example of his premise, Gilfillan
addresses a major problem facing historians, biogra-
phers, and filmmakers trying to present a veracious West
in the presence of a pantheon of heroes and heroines
widely accepted and praised. On the other hand,
Gilfillan stops far short of writers who have studied these

cultural artifacts to show how they illustrate changing cultural attitudes about the legendary popular giants of the American past. One might expect, however, that a man who devoted nearly two decades of his life to sheepherding might be ill at ease with a popular culture that too often championed cowboys as righters of all wrongs and upholders of justice. Gilfillan's daily experiences as a rural western worker were at odds with such a hackneyed, reductive view of the American West.

Gilfillan's writings also reveal an extraordinary interest in nature — shifting weather patterns as well as animal life that frequently seem to shape all aspects of the author's life. Particularly aware of the shift of seasons, he repeatedly shows the impact of their transitions on the sheep and himself. Between winter and spring come lambing time and the beginnings of new life on the rangeland, and with these changes the most pressing days in which herders, night men, and others labor around the clock to pair off ewes and their new lambs. Within a few weeks, spring commences, which, Gilfillan notes in *Sheep,* is "by unanimous consent the worst season of all." The appearance of green grass, "the villain of the piece," (p. 62) regenerates the pastures and provides abundant feed for the sheep but also causes them to "go wild" (p. 63). Ewes and lambs scamper from one new clump of grass to another, with the pursuing herder covering more miles than a wind-driven tumbleweed during these long spring days.

Once the heat arrives to scorch the Dakota grasslands, bands of sheep slow down but also stretch the herder's day by grazing in the morning and early evening during cooler times while taking a siesta in any available shade throughout the heat of midday and early afternoon. With fall comes the most relaxing time for the herder. Gilfillan would enthusiastically agree with what was written of Ernest Hemingway: "Best of all he loved the fall." The fall-time shipping of lambs to market, the shortening days, and the warm days and cool nights are refreshing changes from summer. But the winter arrives with a jolt, with its bone-wracking cold and occasional blasting storms. The herder must closely watch his band during these winter days to keep them together and away from prowling wolves and coyotes. Once the storms of January and February are behind the herder, he again thinks of approaching lambing time and the beginning of a new cycle. Gilfillan is at his best in describing these seasonal shifts and their impacts on him and his sheep.

No less interesting are Gilfillan's accounts of the animal life that surrounds him. At the center of these passages, in loving detail, are the extensive descriptions of sheep that share the author's life—in twenty-four-hour days, seven-day weeks, and twelve-month years. Gilfillan admits that his woolly wards often anger him, so much so that he wishes he might place a swift kick to where they once had tails. Their frequent contrariness as mothers, their tendency to follow a leader wherever that Moses might stray, and their outright stupidity are more than enough to prompt any herder to ask for his wages—but most of the time, Gilfillan thinks of his charges as needing his help, so much better to work with than wild-eyed cattle, and as malleable children expecting his care. Although often exasperated and sometimes ready to quit, Gilfillan is forced to admit that herding sheep offers more satisfaction—particularly in the solitude and freedom it affords—than any other work with livestock.

In two chapters of *Sheep* entitled "The Herder's Partners," and "The Herder's Neighbors," Gilfillan describes the importance of dogs and horses to his work as well as the threats of coyotes and wolves. For any herder, especially those working with a band of fifteen hundred or more in either wide-open country, in brushy foothills, or in the mountains, a pair of dependable and obedient sheep dogs are indispensable, not to mention the added comfort of their companionship. Noting these important roles for sheep dogs, Gilfillan provides several refreshing vignettes of dogs integral to his work. The uninitiated might also think a horse would always be a time- and labor-saving animal for the herder. True, horses are useful as pack animals and for pulling the sheep wagon, but the same animals are often ill suited for riding or for quick dashes to head off a stubborn band of sheep. Although the cowboy without a horse may be as useless as a cinematic cowpoke minus his six-gun, most herders—like Gilfillan—do not find horses vital to their work.

In writing of the conflicts between coyotes and wolves and his sheep, Gilfillan, not surprisingly, sides with predator controllers rather than with conservationists of wild animals. He depicts coyotes as killers of sheep whose numbers must be limited through poisoning or hunting. But he does not support those who wish to eliminate coyotes, wolves, and eagles; he has little regard for such wanton killers. Indeed, in the most extensive and intriguing section of *Sheep*—a portion previously published[14]—Gilfillan details the numerous unsuccessful attempts to kill or capture the legendary wolf called Three Toes. Although the wily gray wolf frequently kills not out of hunger but for the joy of slaughter, Gilfillan sympathizes with the animal who outwits his human opponents—though for several years they try to trap, maim, shoot, or poison him. The author makes Three Toes into something of a hero, despite his being a destroyer of the writer's sheep. Gilfillan seems much intrigued with the killer wolf, more so than one would expect for such a deadly opponent.

How does one account for the popularity of *Sheep,* which sold sufficiently well to be reprinted and which has continued to attract readers in later years? Although the answer to this question is neither simple nor entirely clear, one must examine the cultural and ideological currents of the 1920s and 1930s to understand the book's initial appeal. Clearly these decades illustrate an intriguing paradox in American thought and culture. In those years cities in the United States were supplanting rural settlements as the major social organization in the country; Henry Ford and others were supplying Americans with numerous labor-saving machines and devices; Charles Lindbergh's solo flight across the Atlantic seemed to be ushering in a new marriage of men and machines—indeed, most Americans seemed on the verge of moving ideologically as well as socially and economically into a more urban, industrial, and bureaucratic society. Nonetheless large segments of that society betrayed an uneasiness about their surroundings and embraced cultural events and symbols that reflected earlier frontier, rural, and sometimes agricultural patterns of living and thinking. Zane Grey's fictional westerns depicting a preindustrial Wild West, the western films of William S. Hart, Tom Mix, Buck Jones, and Hoot Gibson, the surging interest in western and southern regionalism, and the popularity of dude ranches, rodeos, and pioneer festivals and reconstructions—all these currents illustrated the desires of many Americans to avoid the oncoming urban-industrial society and culture. Instead men and women wanted to hold on to cultural symbols they thought reflected a freer, more individualistic and democratic society.

For these Americans Gilfillan's *Sheep* was an appealing and satisfying return to earlier, seemingly simpler times. Indeed, in several respects, his work was and is timeless—a man with his flock of sheep *in* nature. Machines might barge into this idyllic garden in the form of trucked-in supplies, mechanized sheepshearers, and the railroading of lambs and old ewes to eastern markets, but these interruptions were exceptions to the age-old daily duties of the herder working his flocks in pastoral settings. Gilfillan, with his extensive background and training in early Christian and ancient Grecian and Roman history and mythology, was not unaware of the multiple meanings to be drawn from depictions of the herder as a natural man, as a keeper of flocks. Like Grey's and Max Brand's novels, like the nostalgic status quo ante bellum longings of the southern agrarians who contributed to *I'll Take My Stand* (1930), and like the back-to-the-primitive urgings of artists who flocked to Santa Fe and Taos, New Mexico, in the interwar years, Gilfillan appealed to a popular yearning for less complicated rural times in his extensive and sympathetic descriptions of the blessed country life that

surrounded and nourished him. In this sense *Sheep*
clearly illustrated major cultural-intellectual currents
that washed over many Americans in the 1920s and
1930s.

On several pages of *Sheep* Gilfillan illuminates the
ties between his book and contemporary ideas and
events. He harpoons prohibition, favors the country over
the towns, and refers to the detrimental impacts of the
Ku Klux Klan and automobiles, all the while regaling
his readers with matters of the sheep country. For example, the unquenchable thirst of a hungry young lamb
conjures the image of the "anti-Prohibitionist . . .
[who] does n't care where he gets his drink, as long as he
gets it" (p. 121). For some readers, explicit references to
the events and ideas of the 1920s may seem as scarce as
black sheep and goats among the author's bands, but
each of the allusions provides context for Gilfillan's
extensive commentaries on the diurnal details of
sheepherding.

The changing status of women — an important issue of
the 1920s and the New Deal era — is also a topic of much
interest to Gilfillan. Women's attitudes, girlish actions,
and feminine dress occupy as much space as any subject
exterior to the lamb lot. Sometimes satirical, often humorous, his comments in *Sheep* and in his other published writings on women imply a negative attitude, but
Gilfillan's handling of this topic is more complex than
simply negative. Early on he wonders if the independent
qualities of his aging mare Bess result from her having
"heard about the new freedom of woman." Perhaps, he
continues, "she will be bobbing her mane and tail next"
(p. 59). Moreover, although he admits that it is "idle for

a herder to speculate on what the ladies wear, and immoral to speculate as to why," he nonetheless is convinced that city women "are animated . . . by that spirit of drastic economy that leads them to keep their clothing as near the vanishing point as liberal police regulations will allow" (p. 61). He also muses that the shorn ewe, like the "thoughtful flapper," ought to "wend her way homeward and put on some clothes" (p. 138). If he makes fun of female clothing or the lack thereof, he is also convinced that women are ill suited for herding because they would be far removed from gossip circles—and "can you really picture a woman engaging in an occupation which would leave her more or less in the dark with regard to the doings of even her immediate neighbors?" (p. 155). "Besides," he adds, "the love affairs of the sheep are all carried on with the greatest openness, and there is no room for speculation, innuendo, or scandal" (p. 156). Nor are women at a loss in the game of self-appreciation. The independence of men "is as nothing compared with the independence of a girl in a community where she is at a premium. Women have never been bearish on their charms, but where they conceive that anything like a corner in the market exists, the sky is the limit" (p. 200).

On the other hand, the bachelor Gilfillan finds much about pioneer and farm women to praise. First of all, nearly all are hard working and persevering. "Many a schoolma'am," he writes, "gave proof of the tough fibre of pioneer womanhood by riding horseback forty miles to a dance, and when there taking her only rest during the supper hour" (p. 14). And he knows of farm women who live in a "ten-by-twelve shack" and keep "busy all

the time" with numerous demanding duties (p. 25). Nor
are women cooks paid "even . . . half" what sheepshearers receive, although they worked long and hard to
feed the shearers. After watching how much men in the
West rely on the help of women and yet how inconsider-
ate they are of their women, Gilfillan concludes that "the
complete emancipation of woman has not yet arrived, at
least not this far West" (p. 137).

When Archie's beloved younger sister Emily asked her
brother why he criticized women so roundly in *Sheep*
and his other writings, he provided ambiguous answers
much like the mixture of negative and positive responses
noted above. He told Emily that a woman — especially as
a wife — would have dominated him and taken away his
freedom, which he cherished more than anything else.
Yet he had to admit that "those who had done most for
him, had been women." Unable to accept a woman as
his wife, he fixed his ideal female as the voluptuous,
ever-young woman of the type who adorned the pinup
calendars in his hotel and apartment rooms. Thus, while
the erotic qualities of young, vivacious women whetted
his sensual desires, he could also praise the hard work of
ranch women like Mrs. Al Dean, the wife of his long-
time boss; but these farm women, his sister Emily con-
cluded, were "kindly ministering angels, and had no
resemblance to the young girls he adored or to the genus
'woman' whom he disliked." The ambivalent attitudes
toward women that Archer betrays in *Sheep* clearly
reflect the personal conflicts that warred within him.[15]

If *Sheep* illuminates ideas of its times and helps illustrate the personal attitudes of the author, it also occupies
a unique niche in the small group of books written about

herders and sheepmen in the American West. Closest in
approach to Gilfillan's book is Hughie Call's *Golden
Fleece,* a lively personal account by a Texas woman who
marries a Montanan and goes to live on his sheep ranch.
A story by an outsider struggling to become an insider,
Call's book pleased Gilfillan, who reviewed it and struck
up a revealing correspondence with its author. Another
volume, *The Golden Hoof* by Winifred Kupper, is a
historical account of sheepraising in the Southwest. A
well-written narrative based on the author's first-hand
experiences and her historical research, the volume is not
so much about herders as about the sheep business of the
region. Much closer to *Sheep* in perspective is Robert
Laxalt's *Sweet Promised Land,* a lovingly remembered
and revealing novelized biography of the Basque
author's sheepherding father. In stressing ethnic backgrounds and conflicts with other ranchers and sheepmen, Laxalt's volume, although a smoothly written and
appealing work, lacks some of the autobiographical
immediacy of Gilfillan's *Sheep.* Finally, well-known
western writer Mary Austin also described herders' experiences in southern California in her book *The Flock.*[16]
Gilfillan, however, much disliked her book, writing in
his unpublished diary: "I see no reason to change my first
opinion of it. There is page after page of pure bullshit.
She never uses one word if she can use ten to express the
same idea."[17]

   Although *Sheep* remains the best first-person account
of a western sheepherder, the book is not a thorough
guide to all aspects of sheepherding throughout the
American West. Gilfillan, for example, makes no mention of the much-utilized transhumant pattern of other

western sheepmen, who trailed or transported their bands from winter and spring ranges to nearby mountains during summer months to take advantage of verdant high-country meadows. Nor does he write about the difficulties of dealing with brushy mountain areas and bears that plagued herders during these summer months. Generally, most other western herders experienced a good deal of varied terrain and landscape during their twelve-month years, certainly more than Gilfillan describes.

Other topics are not broached in *Sheep*. For instance, Gilfillan does little with the selective breeding so important to many sheepmen in the West. One would not know, either, how significant vacations and stays at the home ranch were to many herders. This writer, growing up on a ten-thousand-acre sheep ranch in the Pacific Northwest, remembers the eagerness with which many herders traded their tiresome jobs on the range or in the mountains for a short stay in town or a few days at the home place. Other western sheepmen might also disagree with the author's conclusion that eastern ewes bore twins more often than those in the West. These omissions and differences of opinion are exceptions, however. Most readers of *Sheep* who have herded or raised sheep will experience a shock of recognition in sensing how much that Gilfillan says and does mirrors their backgrounds.

At the same time, the narrator of *Sheep* is an appealing person. He seems to know everything about sheepherding, fills his narrative with interesting stories and examples, and—above all—has a keen sense of humor. In addition, he knows how to include readers without alienating them. As he writes early on, "you could not fire a shotgun into the average crowd in the range country without hitting a man who had at some time herded sheep, but it would probably take the charge in the other barrel to make him admit it" (p. 5). Or, consider his picturesque description of a farm acquaintance, Old Man Shiflet, "a meek, undersized individual, with a large family and two hundred pounds of fighting wildcat for a wife" (p. xli).

The direct, masculine prose of *Sheep* suggests a strong, self-confident author, but the credible narrative persona is all the more remarkable because he is at such odds with the image of Gilfillan contained in his cipher diary and in the recollections of his family and his close personal friends. One scholar succinctly summarizes the clear disparities between the public and private Gilfillan: *Sheep* gives one the impression that its "author is a rough, keenly observant, high-spirited outdoorsman. The diary presents a different personality. He is impractical, insecure, kind, weak, and extraordinarily sensitive."[18]

Finally, the author leaves one with an overwhelming sense of the large and appealing freedoms available in the West. Although Gilfillan does not mention the writings of famous western historian Frederick Jackson Turner, his conclusions are those of that well-known savant: the West is the breeding ground of individualism, democracy, and freedom. Indeed, in the final pages of *Sheep* Gilfillan celebrates the region to which he had fled as a young man and in which he lived most of his life.

By the 1930s, then, *Sheep* was recognized as an

authoritative, appealing account of sheepherding. It remains a classic of the western American livestock indus-
try because it fills a unique place among the handful of
notable books about herding. *Sheep* is the place to begin
to gain an understanding of the life of a western
sheepherder.

RICHARD W. ETULAIN

Center for the American West
University of New Mexico

NOTES

1. The best source of biographical information on Gilfillan is
the forty-three-page unpublished typescript by his sister Emily
Dean Heilman. Entitled "The Story of Archer B. Gilfillan," this
manuscript is in the Archer Gilfillan Collection, Manuscripts Di-
vision, University of Minnesota Libraries, St. Paul, Minnesota.
Also see Austin J. McLean, "A Herder's Life in South Dakota: The
Cipher Diary of Archer B. Gilfillan," in Arthur S. Huseboe and
William Geyer, eds., *Where the West Begins: Essays on Middle
Border and Siouxland Writing, in Honor of Herbert Krause*
(Sioux Falls, S.Dak.: Center for Western Studies, Augustana Col-
lege, 1978), 63–71.

2. Heilman, "Story of Archer B. Gilfillan," 2–10. Gilfillan
speaks of being a "sissy" in his Cipher Diary, vol. 1, 1925
[*sic*]–1927, typescript p. 4, Box 1, Gilfillan Collection.

3. Heilman, "Story of Archer B. Gilfillan," 13. The following
paragraphs draw heavily on this source for biographical information.

4. Gilfillan, *Sheep* (Boston: Little, Brown, and Co., 1929), xliii. Subsequent page references to *Sheep* are cited in the text.

5. Maurice Kildare has written a series of brief biographical sketches of Gilfillan, which include most of these details. Some are, however, at odds with the facts presented in Heilman, "Story of Archer B. Gilfillan." See Kildare, "Gilfillan Enjoyed Herder's Full, Independent Life," *Aberdeen* (South Dakota) *American News,* June 12, 1966, p. 19; "Secret Sorrows of a Sheepherder," *Old West* 2 (Spring 1966): 38–39, 82; "Some Men Need It Lonely," *Old West* 3 (Fall 1966): 57, 73; "The Lonely Shepherd," *National Woolgrower* 57 (February 1967): 32–33, 37; "Sheepherder's Home," *Relics* 7 (Spring 1968): 14–16. All quotes from Gilfillan's diary are in McLean, "A Herder's Life in South Dakota," 70.

6. Untitled and undated clipping in Gilfillan alumni files, University of Pennsylvania Archives, Philadelphia.

7. "The Old Timer," *See America First* 6 (June 1920): 29–31, 40; "Wild Animal Neighbors of the Prairies," *See America First* 6 ([July?] 1920): 18–20, 42, 48; "The Sheep Herder," *Saturday Evening Post,* September 15, 1924, p. 56, 58.

8. Cipher Diary, vol. 1, p. 1, Gilfillan Collection; McLean, "A Herder's Life in South Dakota." McLean has edited and introduced a brief section of Gilfillan's translated cipher diary as "A Sheepherder Out of His Element," *South Dakota Review* 14 (Winter 1976–77): 73–85.

9. Heilman, "Story of Archer B. Gilfillan," 19. Two years after the publication of *Sheep,* Gilfillan recorded in his diary that the appearance of the book was "the most important day of my life," quoted in McLean, "A Sheepherder Out of His Element," 73.

10. Archer B. Gilfillan, *A Shepherd's Holiday, Being the Reflections of a Herder* ([Custer, S.Dak.]: Chronicle Shop, 1936); *A Goat's Eye View of the Black Hills* (Rapid City, S.Dak.: Dean & Dean Publishers, 1953).

11. *New York Times,* November 10, 1929, p. 3; *Wilson Library Bulletin* 25 (December 1929): 41; *Books,* February 23, 1930, p. 18.

12. "The Hero of the Westerns" and "The Cowboy of the Pulps," *A Shepherd's Holiday,* 26–27. Some of the same topics are discussed in Gilfillan, "The Real Cowboy" and "The Western Movie," *South Dakota Review* 4 (Summer 1966): 67–72.

13. Gilfillan, "Calamity Jane — Fact and Fiction," *A Goat's Eye View,* 19–23.

14. "The End of the Killer," *Farm and Fireside,* September 1926, p. 6–7, 64–65.

15. Heilman dealt at length with her older brother's ambivalent attitudes toward women and his sexual insecurities in "Story of Archer B. Gilfillan," 2–3, 7, 8a, 11–13, 16–17, and especially 36–37b, from which the quotations are taken. In a revealing exchange of letters with Hughie Florence Call, author of *Golden Fleece,* Archer wrote that he liked to "razz the women," but he admitted that tendency came "unconsciously from the fact that I never had any success with them." Gilfillan to Hughie Call, March 1, 1944, Hughie Call Collection, Box 1, University of Oregon, Special Collections, Eugene, Oregon.

16. Call, *Golden Fleece* (Boston: Houghton Mifflin Co., 1942); Kupper, *The Golden Hoof: The Story of the Sheep of the Southwest* (New York: Alfred A. Knopf, 1945); Laxalt, *Sweet Promised Land* (New York: Harper and Row, 1957); Austin, *The Flock* (Boston: Houghton Mifflin, 1906). See Gilfillan's letters to Call, October 16, November 12, 27, December 19, 1942, December 29, 1943, and March 1, 1944, Hughie Call Collection. He told Call that Austin's book *The Flock* was "not remarkable for [its] treatment," Gilfillan to Call, October 16, 1942. His review of Call's *Golden Fleece* is contained in his letter of November 12, 1942, to her.

17. Quoted in McLean, "A Herder's Life in South Dakota," 66.

18. Gilfillan's sense of inadequacy, his difficulties with alcohol, and his unattractive physical features are abundantly clear in Heilman, "Story of Archer B. Gilfillan," and in McLean, "A Herder's Life in South Dakota." The quote is from McLean, 67.

If thou dislik'st the Piece thou light'st on first;
Thinke that of All, that I have writ, the worst:
But if thou read'st my Booke unto the end,
And still do'st this, and that verse, reprehend:
O Perverse man! If All disgustfull be,
The Extreame Scabbe take thee, and thine, for me.

ROBERT HERRICK

PREFACE

SOME years ago a book was published under the title, *How the Other Half Lives*. The present volume is not so ambitious in scope. It aims to tell how a much less than prohibition fraction of one per cent lives, a tiny group in comparison with the whole, and yet leading a life so strange as to set it off from even its immediate neighbors. In other words, this book attempts to shed light on the question: "Why is a sheep herder, and How?"

The use of the first personal pronoun is unavoidable in a book of this sort, founded as it is on personal experience, and illuminated with facts.

To reassure those who think that a herder is necessarily so ignorant that whatever he may write is negligible, let me hasten to add that this book is my *magnum opus*, the *apologia pro vita mea*, and my *terminus ad quem*.

A friend of mine, a herder of long standing, recently said to me, "The longer you herd, the less you know!" Gazing earnestly upon his honest and once intelligent face, I could not but feel that he spoke the truth, and that I should be taking undue chances in putting off any longer the task I had set myself. So, by the light of the last flickering gleams of intelligence, I am going to set down these few random thoughts on herding, trusting that I may be able to finish while the candle is yet burning, and before it gutters out into utter darkness.

BUFFALO, SOUTH DAKOTA
January 18, 1928

PROLOGUE

I COME of a literary family. My grandfather, a minister, wrote a book on *The Origin of Sin;* but people were apparently not as much interested in the origin of sin as they were in the daily practice of it, and the book was not a commercial success. My father, also a minister, likewise wrote a book; but he was too intrinsically good a man to write a really popular novel. So far from giving the public what it wanted, he believed that the public should be restrained from what it wanted; and so his book was not a financial success either. And now my nieces are getting ink on their fingers, one of them having won a prize in a magazine essay contest and the other being guilty of several indiscretions in her high-school paper. So apparently it is a family taint, ineradicable and incurable.

All my life I have been interested in sheep. When as a boy I made my first considerable accumulation, — namely, three dollars, — I spent it in the purchase of a good ewe and left her on the farm where I had summered. The next year the ewe with her wool and her lamb brought me six dollars. Greatly encouraged, I added to this three dollars from another source and bought three ewes and left them on the same farm. The next fall I found myself worth eighteen dollars. While I had never been especially good at mathematics, it seemed to me that 100 per cent a year was a pretty good return on an investment, and that if I could keep it up regularly I ought to be worth quite a bit some day. So I bought as many ewes as I had money for, and left them, supposedly on shares, with a neighboring farm woman who had a few sheep of her own. For some reason or other I did not return to this region the following year, and then it was that I discovered the sorrows of absentee ownership and the perfidy of woman. For this particular daughter of Eve mailed my mother a check for ten dollars, which she claimed represented the difference between the value of my sheep and the amount of the pasture bill she had against them. And I learned about women from her. I was wiped out. But while women are man's ineradicable weakness, sheep are not ; and it was many a year before I again took up the trail of the Golden Hoof. From the other trail there *is* no turning aside.

When I was a boy I had a real fondness for physical labor. This feeling has since perceptibly diminished. But when I was in my teens, while the family spent the summer at the mountains or the seashore, I would go by preference to some farm and put in two or three months at work. The first two summers were spent on a farm in Virginia, and, although I did a boy's work and put in the same time as the men, I received no pay and was thoroughly and completely happy. The third summer was spent on a sixteen-acre farm in Massachusetts. The owner of it said that a man who could n't make a living off four acres was no farmer. He might have added that a man who could do that was no farmer either, but a truck gardener. I did not like the town, and I used to repeat to myself with great relish the lines of Poe : —

And when, amid no earthly moans,
  Down, down that town shall settle hence,
Hell, rising from a thousand thrones,
  Shall do it reverence.

It seemed to me that the poet had stated the case much more powerfully and accurately than I could hope to do. When fall and school time drew near, the farmer told me that I had been a good boy and gave me five dollars for my summer's wages.

The following year I worked on a farm in Pennsylvania, and when I say "worked" I mean just that. We got up every morning at half-past four, milked twenty-seven cows before breakfast, and I stirred the milk to cool it while the rest ate. Then we put in a full day's work in the field, had a somewhat early supper, and then milked the twenty-seven cows all over again. We were usually through by eight o'clock at night. When I drew my pay in the fall, the boss said in an aggrieved tone, "You said that wages was n't no object," and he proved the sincerity of his belief in my words by giving me twelve dollars for my summer's work. It may be seen at once that the money end of it was not what attracted me to farm work.

But if the time spent on the farm did not yield large financial returns, I was richly rewarded in other ways. In the field hands that worked on the Virginia farm I found the most real and genuine people I have ever known before or since. They had neither the wit nor the desire to be

anyone on this green footstool but themselves.
That was thirty years ago, and yet their portraits remain undimmed to this day. There
was Bryant, a long, gangling man whose marriage had been blessed with no sons, but to whom
Nature had by way of compensation given seven-
teen daughters, of whom several of the older
were married and the youngest just walking.
There was the top hand, Pomp McCauley, bald-
headed, cross-looking, and thoroughly kind-
hearted, who could do with horses and machinery anything that any other man could do.
Then there was Old Man Shiflet, a meek, undersized individual, with a large family and two
hundred pounds of fighting wildcat for a wife.
He had the perpetual look of one to whom everything that could happen had happened, and for
whom anything that might happen in the future
would be of no consequence.

From these men and their families I learned
quite a little biology, considerable assorted language, and somewhat of human nature "as is."
They were genuine and they were real. Why
is it that the further we advance in civilization,
the more we wrap ourselves about with strand
after strand of protective filament, until we finally become and remain mere perambulating
cocoons, with whatever life is left in us going

on beneath the surface ? The worm and butterfly stages may have their drawbacks, but at least they are preferable to the drab uniformity of the cocoons.

I spent my college vacations in charge of the boys at a Fresh Air camp. The work was congenial and the pay much higher than on the farm. It was here that I received an impulse in favor of one of the two courses of action that have divided my life. As the son of a minister and with relatives in social-service work, I had a strong desire to be of some service to my fellow man. I had also the strong desire of every normal adolescent to make something of myself — in other words, to succeed. When I left the university the second of the two impulses was in the ascendant. I had taken all the Latin and Greek I could in college, partly from a natural liking for the ancient languages, and partly because I wished to have a possible teaching subject to fall back on, much as an aviator straps a parachute on his back, with faith in its efficacy, but with a fervent prayer that it may not be needed. My desire was toward a stockman's life, and immediately upon graduation I set out for the West, to unlock the gate of riches with a Phi Beta Kappa key.

I headed for a cattle country, although I had

then and still have as much business around a
bunch of cattle as I have around a high-powered
racing plane. After a few months' hay pitching on a cattle ranch and a winter's work on a
farm, I contracted a severe case of land fever.
Since the only known cure for this disease is to
take up a homestead, that is what I did, settling
about a hundred miles north of the Black Hills
near the Slim Buttes of Harding County, in
the northwest corner of the state. After being
on the homestead a year, I persuaded my father
that I was ready to begin my life work, and I
invested every cent of the patrimony he gave
me in a bunch of sheep, and thus automatically
became a sheepman. But that is not the way
sheepmen are made.

It is my belief that a few, and a very few, of
us are meant to work for ourselves, and that the
vast majority of us are meant to work for someone else. It cost me everything I had in the
world to learn that I belonged in the second
group. There is no use going into the painful
details; suffice it to say that in three years
from the time I left college I was practically
broke. Under these circumstances it is not surprising that the other of the two impulses which
have always remained with me should have
asserted itself, and that I should have become

convinced that I had a call to a life of service. The world of business was dust and ashes in my mouth, and the shining heights of self-sacrifice beckoned me on. I entered a theological seminary.

The three years that I spent in that institution saw a gradual but steady growth of disbelief in the entire theological structure of the church for whose ministry I was studying. On the eve of graduation I realized that I could never conscientiously take the ordination vows, and I did the only possible thing under the circumstances, and withdrew. Since some of my friends somewhat more than hinted that my exit was not entirely voluntary, I hastily gathered together some papers proving the contrary, put them in a safe, and have changed the combination twice a week ever since.

Not wishing to go home while at a loose end for the second time since graduation, I came back to the place where I had homesteaded. Having always been a hearty eater and wishing to continue this pleasant practice, I took the first job that offered, which happened to be sheep herding. The question in my mind was whether or not I should study for the ministry of the church to which I had been attracted. I had already made two costly mistakes: the first had annihilated my patrimony and the second had taken three years out of my life. I made up my mind that I would take at least a year to think things over. That was thirteen years ago, and I am still thinking them over.

When the average student leaves college, he does not simply *feel* invincible, he *knows* that he is. The heights before him do not daunt him in the least, and toward the figures on their shining summits he feels a friendly interest, as of one who will soon be there beside them. As the trail roughens and unexpected pitfalls disclose themselves, he aims at ever lower and lower peaks. And in the end, with heights unscaled and depths unplumbed, he plods with more or less contentment with myriad millions of his fellow men along the dusty plain, and his lot becomes the general lot of human kind — flashes of joy and sorrow, and the rest humdrum.

And so, having reached no eminence whatever, but merely a pleasant patch of shade in a green meadow, I should like to sit down awhile and look forward and back — and around.

SHEEP

I

HERDING AND HERDERS

IN fairness to the reader it should be stated at the outset that there are two general theories about herding. Some hold that no man can herd for six months straight without going crazy, while others maintain that a man must have been mentally unbalanced for at least six months before he is in fit condition to entertain the thought of herding. Since these theories, taken together, hold out little hope for the steady herder, I ask the reader, in case he should notice any irrationality in the following pages, to impute it to environment rather than heredity. It is easier on the family.

To a mind uncontaminated by the Higher Criticism, the herding profession as personified in the second son of Adam holds a very high and honorable rank in point of antiquity. In fact, the herder stands next to the very head of the procession, while the wealthy radio manufacturer brings up the rear, with the hairpin manufacturer dropped out, and the corset maker groggy. It is significant that the first herder was killed by his brother. The prejudice against sheep is evidently as old as the profession itself. But Abel was lucky at that ; for if Cain, instead of being a farmer, had been a cattleman, he not only would have killed Abel, but would afterward have skinned him and tacked his hide on the barn door as a warning to all other herders.

Time does strange things to us and ours. It transmutes the artistic excrescence of yesterday into the treasured heirloom of to-day, and on the other hand it makes the world's champion pugilist of to-day the has-been of to-morrow. But time has dealt hardest of all with the herder. From a high and honorable place in the pastoral ages he has gradually descended, until in this age of industrialism he has only one consolation left, and that is the secure knowledge that he is working on rock bottom, that no matter what he does he never can get any lower, and that any time he makes a change in his occupation he will automatically rise in the social scale. You could not fire a shotgun into the average crowd in the range country without hitting a man who had at some time herded sheep, but it would probably take the charge in the other barrel to make him admit it. About the only person who isn't ashamed to admit having herded is a sheepman, and he refers to it merely to show how far he has come.

It was not always so. Jacob herded sheep and then married his boss's daughter, although it took him seven years to talk the old man into it. Not only that, but he became the father of a race that have demonstrated their ability to live and thrive in any part of the world but Scotland, where they regularly get stranded and starve to death unless rescued by their more wary brethren. But Jacob's descendants don't herd sheep. No, they have progressed onward and upward.

And yet the herder, even to-day, has distant relatives, ninety-third cousins, as it were, in the higher ranks of life, for every pastor of a church is by his very name and profession a shepherd or herder. But if it would not be presumptuous, it might be pointed out that the sheep herder has some advantages over even his wealthy and aristocratic kinsman. In the first place the herder can tell his black sheep at a glance, which is something no pastor can do. Furthermore, the herder does n't lie awake nights wondering how he can turn his black sheep white. He has sense enough to know that they will remain black to the end of the chapter. Nor does he worry for fear that his black sheep will smudge up some of the white ones, turning them a rich mulatto. Besides all this, the herder's black sheep will average only about one to the hundred. Where is the pastor who can boast a score like that? Lastly, when the whole flock shows a tendency to go wrong, as it frequently does, the herder does n't tearfully beg it to go right, and get in another herder to work over it a week or two. No, he addresses his flock in short, concise phrases. He alludes in passing to certain interesting facts about their ancestry, touches briefly on the present state of their morals, winds up with a reference to their hoped-for destination, and then sets the dog on them. The pastor has certain inhibitions of speech ; the herder has none unless he is tongue-tied, and few of them are. But, after all, the herder and the pastor speak much the same language, only differently arranged.

It is necessary, however, to differentiate between the sheep herder of fact and the shepherd of romance. The latter is a gay and poetic figure, the former anything but. The shepherd leads his flock with a song, the herder follows his with profanity. The shepherd reclines on a mossy bank beneath a green tree and carols a roundelay. The herder looks carefully about to make sure that he won't sit on a cactus, eases his wearied limbs to the unshaded hillside, and gives his vocal organs a well-earned rest.

But to descend from the shepherd of romance to the shepherd of fact, there is still a great difference between him and the sheep herder — roughly speaking, about a thousand dollars a year. The shepherd, in modern life, is the man who has charge of a comparatively small band of pure-bred sheep. He tells the hired man what to give them, and he tells the boss what to give him. The sheep herder is in charge of a large band of sheep, but he does n't tell anybody anything. If he has anything to say, he tells it to the sheep.

There is another marked difference between the shepherd and the sheep herder. It is best told in the words of an old Scotch herder in Montana. He said that in the old country, when he drove his band of sheep down to the lower pastures at

the approach of winter, people would exclaim,
"Here comes the noble shepherd and his flock!"
Out here, on the other hand, when they saw
him coming they would say, "Here comes that
low-lived herder and his bunch of woolies!"

In Biblical times the owner of flocks was a
nomad. He had his herdsmen, but he moved
with them from place to place as the need for
fresh grass dictated, taking with him his family
and all he possessed. To-day the sheep owner
is as stationary as any corn-belt farmer, but the
herder is still a nomad. A band of sheep will
take all the feed within a reasonable distance
in about a month or six weeks. Then they
must be moved to fresh pastures. Since
the ranch buildings are usually situated near
the centre of the sheepman's range and since the
sheep swing aroung the edges of the range in the
course of a year, the herder may be likened to a
planet swinging around its central sun, which at
highly irregular intervals gives off gleams of
gold, or silver, or I O U's, as the case may be,
said gleams having the force of gravity in keeping the herder swinging in his orbit. All this
necessitates a high degree of mobility for the
herder and his belongings, and the answer to this
is the sheep wagon, the most comfortable home a
bachelor could desire.

But before describing this, it ought to be said that not all herders have a wagon.   In fact, there are many different kinds of herding.   There is herding from the ranch, for example, which means that the herder lives in the ranch buildings, takes the sheep out to graze during the day, and returns them to the corral at night.   Most herders have a taste of this sometime during the year, usually during the winter.   Some herders are on government reserves and have to bed their sheep in a different spot every night, and have a pack horse with which to carry their bed and provisions from place to place.   In some parts of the country the herder has a team hobbled out near the wagon and does his own camp tending, that is, gets his own provisions, by the novel method of propping up the forward end of his wagon, detaching the front half of the running gears, and jogging away comfortably to where his provisions await him.   But in most places a herder caught trying to take the front wheels off his wagon would quickly receive free transportation to some state institution where he would be assigned to a small but well-upholstered room and given a toy wagon which he might take apart to his heart's content.

Again there is a great difference in the kind of country herded over.   There is mountain herding and plains herding, and there is herding on wooded slopes. But to herders who cannot keep track of all their sheep on the open prairie, it must ever remain a mystery how a herder can keep track of any of them in the woods, where he will not see the whole bunch together from one day's end to the other.

But as human nature is much the same, whether seen in a village bazaar in India or a bizarre village in New York, so sheep nature is doubtless sheep nature the world over, and herders all over the West have much the same problems to solve, much the same life to live, whether they herd on the mountains or on the plains, or in the depths of the forest. And wherever he is, the herder is the foundation stone of the sheep business or the bottom rung of the social ladder. It all depends on the point of view.

II

SHEEP COUNTRY

When the white man with his superior civilization and his superiority complex took this continent from his red brother, he gave back to him certain patches of land here and there, together with an urgent invitation to make his home on these and not elsewhere. At that time the white man did not know that Nature had slipped a joker into the deck in the form of certain hidden oil pools, and by the time he found that out he was in a position where he could afford himself the luxury of a conscience, and so he magnanimously decided to let the tail go with the hide. The reservation system resulted in the damming here and there of the westward flood of migration. One such barrier against which the human flood heaped itself was the large Indian reservation on the west bank of the Missouri

River midway of the State of South Dakota, containing the historic spot at the mouth of Grand River where Sitting Bull, the greatest of the Sioux, met his destined and still-debated end. North of this reservation the advancing tide swept along the route marked out by the Milwaukee and the Northern Pacific, and south of it traffic had long flowed to the Black Hills. But directly west of it was an eddy, a scantly inhabited region of big cattle outfits, a land which remained, except for the substitution of cattle for buffalo, in the same state in which the ages had left it till as late as the year 1909.

This, at least, is one theory employed to explain the fact that the northwestern corner of South Dakota was an untouched wilderness less than twenty years ago, and in any argument as to the location of the much-discussed Last Frontier this region has at least the right to be considered. But the fact that it was not settled did not mean that it had no history of its own. It lay on the outskirts of the battle that was waged for the possession of the Black Hills. The last of the huge northern herd of buffalo were said to have been slaughtered on its western edge, along the banks of the Little Missouri River. And some sixty miles north along this historic stream is the region made famous for all time by

Theodore Roosevelt and the Marquis de Mores, and beautified for all time by Nature in those Bad Lands which are soon to become a national park.

Following the early period of the big outfits, there came the nesters. A cowboy working for one of the big cattle companies would spot some particularly desirable location for a ranch, would file on it, and start to build up a herd of his own. Sometimes when the growth of his bunch of cattle was phenomenally rapid, the big owners perhaps might say of him sorrowfully, as we are wont to do of the departed, "His gain is our loss." Gradually the big outfits were squeezed out or voluntarily abandoned the field, and the nester, now called the old-timer, inherited the land.

Then came a sort of Golden Age, to which every old-timer looks back with reverence and longing. In spite of his name, time really meant very little to him at all. If he did not see a particular bunch of cattle one day, he could see them some other day — or the following week, for that matter. He knew all his neighbors from one railroad to the other, a distance of a hundred and fifty miles. The ranches were located so far apart that there was very little range trouble. No man could go to the next ranch and return before mealtime, and so a man ate wherever he happened to be, and hospitality was the rule. Dances that were scheduled for one night only, and all night according to custom, might be prolonged for several days by storms or the impassable condition of such roads as there were. And many a schoolma'am gave proof of the tough fibre of pioneer womanhood by riding horseback forty miles to a dance, and when there taking her only rest during the supper hour.

The peaceful serenity of this existence not only was shattered, but overwhelmed and all but obliterated, by a tidal wave of homesteaders that swept across the prairies from the east, and left in its wake a shack, dugout, or sod shanty on every quarter section. Sometimes the old-timer would try to sweep back the sea with his broom, sometimes he was wiped out of existence, but in many cases the ranch that he built up still remains, an island washed by an alien flood. For the homesteader was of a different breed altogether, and in spite of twenty years of association the two types remain distinct to this day. The homesteader could never comprehend the easygoing ways of the old-timer, and the latter in turn never will be able to understand the psychology of a man who, in answer to a knock, could come to the door of his shack busily masticating a mouthful of his dinner, answer the stranger's questions with regard to the road, and then shut his door and return to his meal without having asked the other if he had eaten.

Although the nesters almost without exception were cattlemen to begin with, there came to be a sprinkling of sheepmen among them. There never was in this region the deadly hatred between the two kinds of stockmen that led to a reign of terror in the region farther west. As cattle fell and sheep rose in price, more and more cattlemen were converted. With the influx of the homesteaders, the cattlemen were still further embarrassed; while the sheepmen, with their personally conducted flocks, were able to adapt themselves to the new conditions more readily. For a time the balance was about even, but now the cattlemen are in the minority, and the print of the Golden Hoof is seen all over the land.

There are several factors which make this region preëminently a stock country. The distance at which it lies from the railroad puts a premium on that form of production which can negotiate the long and difficult journey on its own four legs. The cheapness of the land renders large holdings possible to men of even moderate means. And the peculiarities of the climate make the winter feeding of stock particularly easy.

The grass in the East is apt to be much more luxuriant than that of the West, and it grows all summer long. The farmer of the East may or may not figure on forty cows to the acre, but the cattleman of the West used to figure on forty acres for the support of one cow the year round. Even at that, though, the western stockman's grass was better for all-year feed. The grass of the East grows all summer and freezes green in the fall, and from then on is practically useless for stock purposes until its rejuvenation in the spring. The grass on the prairies of the West has a short growing season. By August the prairies are brown. But that same August sun has cured the grass and made hay of it right where it grew. The stockman gathers enough of this hay for his barn use or as much as he has the help to put up. But the millions of tons of it that he cannot handle his stock contentedly harvest for him during the winter months, when the much objurgated wind has swept the ridges bare. And if there is an open winter, that is, one with little snow, his stock will come through rolling fat and he will be able to save his hay stacks for another year. The combination of summer sun and winter wind provides him with an abundance of hay, and his stock attends to putting it up for him.

Although this region is included in what the old geographies used to call the Great American Desert, it is hard to see how it could ever have deserved that name. There is abundance of grass everywhere, and enough running water to supply the needs of stock. True, the rainfall is somewhat light, as was discovered by the stranger passing through the country who stopped to talk with a homesteader leaning against his shack. In the course of the conversation he asked, "Have you had any rain here lately?" "I don't know," was the languid response, "I have only been here three years."

When we speak of the West as a new country, we usually mean in point of settlement and civilization. But this region is new geologically as well. Here are strange sights never seen east of the Mississippi — mud buttes standing solitary like the solidified cores of mud volcanoes, cut banks with bare perpendicular walls of earth exposed, deep draws like gashes cut in the ground with some giant's knife, and so-called Bad Lands with their weird formation and fantastic coloring. In the East the lines of the landscape are softened and rounded; in the West they are sharp and crude.

Owing to the altitude, the air is so light that hills which are miles away stand out against the sky with knife-like clearness. People who come here from the East are invariably fooled as to distances. They have always associated clearness with nearness, and sometimes they learn the difference to their sorrow. An old-timer told me how, when he first came here, he tried out a new rifle on the slopes of Bear Butte and was much disappointed at not seeing the dust fly from it. He learned later that the butte was many miles away. They tell a story of a stranger who set out one morning to walk to a certain butte before breakfast. He walked a mile or two and then met a native who told him that the butte was still several miles away, so he decided to return. They traveled by a slightly different route and came to a small stream, a mere trickle across the sand. As the native stopped to water his horse, he was amazed to see the stranger busily stripping off his clothes. "What are you going to do?" he asked. "I'm going to swim this river," was the dogged response. "Swim it!" ejaculated the native. "Why, you can step across it!" "Well, I don't know," was the cautious answer. "Distances are deceiving in this country, and I'm not taking any chances."

Six miles from the ranch buildings, at the eastern edge of the range over which I herd, rise

the white cliffs of the Slim Buttes, a high range
of hills starting abruptly from the surrounding
plain.   Halfway to the top is a small bench, upon
which is a spring capable of watering hundreds of
cattle.   This bench is the site of an old ranch
called "The Moonshine," a ranch that goes back
to the days of free grass and big outfits.   As you
stand on a hill above where the log ranch house
lay, you find yourself in a natural amphitheatre.
Behind you the rock-strewn earth rises almost
sheer to the plateau, two hundred feet above
you.   To the north a great white limestone wall
thrusts out into space, its rough sides forming
many a niche for an eagle's nest, and its jagged
top their favored resting place.   To the south
a grass-covered, pine-clad shoulder reaches out
like another protecting arm, with a giant pine
crowning a knoll at its very tip ; and below it a
sheer upthrust of limestone wall is pierced by a
roughly shaped window.   Almost at your feet,
nestling among the rough hummocks of the
bench, is the Moonshine Lake, a bright jewel
in a waterless landscape.

As your eyes go farther afield, you note that
from the bench the land drops away another
hundred feet or so to the plain beneath.   Twenty
miles to the northwest you see the large rolling
outlines of the Cave Hills, while thirty miles

west are the white-cliffed, pine-clad summits of
the Short Pine Hills. Beyond them, a mere
blue line, are the Long Pine Hills of Montana.
As your eye follows the horizon south, it pauses
at the Crow Buttes, where the Crow and Sioux
Indians once fought a bloody battle, and at the
twin peaks, Castle Rock and Square Top, rising
in solitary state above many a flat and weary mile
of gumbo. And just beyond them, you see on
the horizon what looks like a row of rounded blue
hummocks. These are the Black Hills, one
hundred miles from where you are standing.

But just as one swallow does not make a
summer, so one view, however enchanting, does
not make an unusual landscape. There are,
however, scattered over the face of the country,
innumerable sharply rising hills or peaks, called
buttes. From the top of any of these the herder
may watch his sheep spread out below him peacefully grazing. He may watch the alternate sun-
light and shadow chase each other over twenty
miles of prairie. A car crawls lazily along a distant road. Out on the horizon a row of jagged
peaks reveals a more pretentious range of hills.
The sky seems to come down to shoulder height
all around. Strange it would be if the all-pervading calm did not bring with it an interior
peace.

III

THE SHEEP WAGON

PICTURE to yourself the old Conestoga wagon or prairie schooner, shorten it somewhat, widen it to extend out over the wheels, pull the canvas taut and smooth so that there will be no ribbed appearance, put a small window in the back and a door in the front — and there you have the herder's happy home. There is a short length of stovepipe sticking up through the canvas on one side near the front. You will notice that the door is not placed squarely in the middle, but toward the opposite side from the stovepipe. The door itself is unusual. It is built in two halves, one above, one below, and each half swings independently on its own hinges. In the upper half are three small windowpanes in a vertical line. How much light they admit depends upon how recently they have been installed, because of course the herder is a herder and not a window washer by profession. The usual explanation for the divided door is that it permits the wagon to be ventilated without cooling off the stove. But I think that is only part of it. It is really the most convenient thing imaginable. You may want to keep the dog in or out without keeping the door shut, so you close the lower half. Also, if you open the full door, the effect is somewhat like opening one entire side of a house. But by keeping the bottom half closed you prevent floor drafts, while the top half, being fastened with a chain, may be kept open at any angle desired, thus affording a perfect means of ventilation. The window at the rear is hinged at the top and may be raised or lowered by a rope passing over a pulley and fastened inside the wagon within easy reach. Thus the window also may be held open at any point desired, making the sheep wagon one of the most easily and perfectly ventilated abodes of man.

You get into the wagon by the simple process of stepping on the wagon tongue, grasping the sides of the door, and hoisting yourself in. Some herders use a box or a pair of steps. As you stand in the doorway you have the stove on one hand, with the dish cupboard behind it, and on the other side a bench running from the door to the bed. The latter, built crosswise of the wagon, takes up the last four or five feet of space. Opposite the long bench is a shorter one running from the bed to the dish cupboard. These benches are directly over the wheels. If you examine them closely, you will see a trapdoor in the centre of each, and these lead into the grub boxes. As may be seen from the outside, the grub boxes are suspended in the space between the rear and front wheels, thus carrying out that economy of space which is the keynote of the sheep wagon.

To return to the inside. Hinged to the bed and jutting forward between the two benches is the table. Its forward edge is supported either by a gate leg beneath or by a chain dropped from the framework of the top. In either case the table may be let down and out of the way when not in use. Sometimes it is arranged to slide in and out beneath the bed. There is also quite a space beneath the bed, where the dogs may be out from underfoot and where bulky articles may be kept.

The bed itself is a built-in bunk with sides a foot or more high. Sometimes it has a set of springs resting on its hard board bottom, but more often only a mattress. Sometimes the herder furnishes the bedding, sometimes the boss. Customs vary in different regions. Just above the bed is a small window, mentioned before, through which the herder may look out over his sheep at night without getting up. Over the bed is a shelf or two, where the herder keeps his clothes, books, and papers.

Such in brief is "the wagon," and for the purposes for which it was designed it would seem hard to improve on it. The keynote of it, as said before, is economy of space. The door and window both open out. The top is high enough so that a tall man may stand upright. For one man there is plenty of room; two crowd it; three are unbearable. But it was intended and designed for one.

We hear so much of the number of steps a woman has to take in pursuit of her work. Someone has even computed the number of miles she is compelled to walk daily — that is, around the house and excluding trips to the movies and the barber. Think of this household marathon and then think of being able to stand in one spot to get an entire meal, to take two steps to sit down and eat it, and then to rise in place and wash the dishes. If the efficiency experts once get a good look at a sheep wagon, they will shortly have all the women under canvas. The herder has no upstairs work to do. He sweeps his wagon whenever it needs it, usually twice a day, and he does the scrubbing and dusting every time the Republicans sweep the solid South.

It is a wonder that there are so few women sharing their husbands' lives in a wagon. Think of a woman's being able to get her housework for the day done in fifteen or twenty minutes. That is all the time the herder spends on it. And yet I am not sure it would work out that way. I have known many a woman homesteader to spend the whole day keeping house in a ten-by-twelve shack, and be busy all the time. What she did or could find to do for that length of time must take its place with the great number of other feminine mysteries, as for example why a woman will order a skirt two inches above the knee and then spend nine tenths of her waking hours pulling it down. I have heard women say that it is harder to keep house in a small place than a large one. That is worse than mysterious. It borders on the cryptic and esoteric. On the other hand, we have all heard of "the burden of a large house." That is a woman every time. She gets you going and coming. The man who tries to argue with one is licked before he starts. The wise man does n't try.

A sheepman whom I knew used to say that if he had as good a time in Heaven as the average woman has on earth, he would be perfectly contented. He pointed out that they have a nice warm place to work in during the winter's cold, and an equally nice cool place in summer. It has regretfully to be recorded that he was unable to convert his wife to his views.

Of course, there are some problems connected with housekeeping even in a wagon. For instance, I am in the habit of putting the coffeepot down into the stove to encourage early boiling. Naturally the pot collects a thick coat of soot. The boss claims that a mixture of soap and elbow grease would cause this soot to disappear. I claim that it would n't. The question has not yet been settled. Then there is another problem arising from the fact that the water pail stands directly beneath the mirror, which causes complications. However, there must be some way out of the difficulty, and doubtless in time I shall discover it.

An observant visitor in a wagon would notice that each of the shelves of the dish cupboard has a three-inch strip of wood hinged to its front edge, the strip being equipped with hooks so that the shelf may be converted into an open box at will. He might also notice that the dishes, both cups and plates, are of tin. These little details point significantly to the herder's secret sorrow, to the fly in the amber of his peaceful existence — that is, moving day. An old proverb says that three removes are as bad as a fire. That being so, how would you like, once every month, to pile all your belongings on the bed, have an unsympathetic earthquake attached to the front of the house, and have the aforesaid house dragged over several miles of rough country? Yet this is just what happens to the herder's home. At the end of the journey he may find that the mirror has again been cracked across, or that the kerosene can has been upset on the bed, inducing dreams of oil-stock swindles, or that the syrup pail has tipped over and has spread its contents in a thin veneer over all adjacent objects. All these accidents can and do happen, but a merciful providence usually sees to it that they do not all happen at once; otherwise the suicidal or homicidal rate for the sheep business would be very high. The condition of things at the end of the journey depends largely on the skill and care-fulness of the camp tender, whose business it is to move the wagon.   But a person will always take better care of his own stuff than another will, and some of the camp tenders are stronger in the back than they are north of the ears.   The herder can sometimes do his own packing, if he knows with certainty the day on which he is to be moved, but he can never do the driving, as he has to tend to the sheep.

It would surprise the average person to know how comfortable a sheep wagon is, summer and winter.   Almost everyone knows that the aver-age tent is unbearable on a hot day.   He might think that the sheep wagon, being a tent on wheels, would be the same way.   But such is not the case.   The canvas top is usually of several thicknesses, which renders it impervious to the sun's rays, and with the door open in front and the window open in the rear whatever breeze there is comes through, and unless the stove is going the wagon is cool compared with the outside.   In like manner in winter the many layers of canvas above and the double matched-board floor beneath keep in a surprising amount of heat.   Likewise the fact that there is such a comparatively small air space to heat makes it possible to keep the wagon at a very comfortable temperature.

Many herders are out in their wagons all winter, and this in a country that sees forty below every year, and in which zero weather frequently extends over long periods.

And yet, with all its attractions, the wagon seems to make a very limited appeal to women. It is the great exception, even where the herder is married, that his wife lives with him in the wagon. To be sure, there is really room for only one, but then man and wife are supposed to be one, so that should n't make any difficulty. Of course, there would be no room for temperament, and in case the husband found it advisable or necessary to make a hasty exit he might in his excitement forget about the three-foot drop and break a leg. But whether the reason is prudence on the part of the man or disdain on the part of the woman, the fact is that a wagon with a woman in it is as rare as a tearoom without one, and it seems likely that the wagon will continue to be in the future, as it has been in the past, the refuge of the married man and the hiding place of the bachelor.

When the preacher warned his congregation, "Don't do as I do ; do as I say do," he was merely voicing in another form the sad human experience that there is a vast difference between theory and practice. Nowhere perhaps is this contrast more strongly revealed than in the difference between herding as it might be and herding as it is.

In theory, the herder rises with the dawn, cooks his simple but substantial breakfast, does his few housekeeping tasks, and is ready for the day's work. He gently pushes the sheep off the bed ground, — that is, the place where they have slept, — and they move slowly out on the prairie, keeping well together, grazing steadily towards the place where they will water. The eager and intelligent dog goes this way and that as the herder motions him, working just enough to turn the sheep as desired, but not so fast as to cause them to bunch up. Finally the band arrives at the stream or water hole, drinks there and lies down for an hour or so, while the herder, a short distance away on a hill, eats his lunch and reads a good story. Then the sheep, one after another, begin to graze again, working towards the wagon, filling themselves to bursting with the rich prairie grasses. Seeing that they are headed in the right direction, the herder, in all the calm glory of a prairie sunset, walks slowly on before them and, arriving at the wagon, sets about preparing his evening meal. Behind him the sheep come steadily onward, and sometime before dark graze on to the bed ground and lie down, chewing the cud of fullness and content.

Such days do come, but when one of them occurs the herder puts a red mark on the calendar and neglects to say his prayers.

What is much more likely to happen is this. Just as the herder, who has overslept, begins to eat his breakfast, the sheep leave the bed ground. Of course, he could dog them back to the wagon, but they might leave immediately in the opposite direction. So he takes the other alternative — bolts his breakfast, puts up a hasty lunch, and goes in pursuit. The sheep have only a twenty-minute start, but that is all any bunch of sheep needs. They are almost a mile from the wagon when they are overhauled, with the aid of a long-distance run by the dog. But just as the dog reaches them, he forgets which way he was motioned to turn, and races up the wrong side, throwing them in the opposite direction from that which the herder intended. There is no help for it now, and the herder calls the dog back. The sheep, however, have not yet had their run out, and they start off zestfully in a new direction. They have to be checked again, for there is no point or profit in letting them run all over the country instead of settling down to graze as they ought to do. So the dog is sent again, and once more he checks them in their headlong flight. The sheep are disappointed, but still hopeful, and

they step out in a new direction with an enthusiasm worthy of a much better cause. By
this time the herder is wild-eyed, and is rapidly
becoming hoarse. Instead of sending the dog he
goes around them himself two or three times,
tying them up in a knot and turning them back
as they attempt to break this way and that.
Finally it dawns on whatever the sheep use for a
mind that it is unwise to attempt any more cross-
country runs at the moment, and so they do the
next best thing and settle down to graze, which
they might just as well have done in the first
place.

The herder makes sure that they are settled,
and then goes to the top of the nearest hill with
the idea of taking his weight off his feet. Since
it is nearly noon, and the sheep seem quiet, he
unwraps his hastily prepared and unappetizing
lunch and begins to eat. A brisk wind has
sprung up, and suddenly over a low rise of ground
comes a tumbleweed, or Russian thistle, rolling
over and over and making good time. As it
reaches the outskirts of the bunch the nearest
sheep look up startled, mistake it for the dog, and
promptly run toward the centre of the band.
Each sheep communicates its fright to the next,
and in fifteen seconds they are all in a compact
mass. Then, obeying a common impulse, they

start out again on their travels, in any direction except towards the wagon.

The herder sees them go, but he is eating his lunch and is tired from a morning of steady walking. He decides to wait till he has finished, but he pays dearly for this indulgence. For by the time he has wiped his mouth with the back of his hand the sheep have not only traveled quite a distance, but have split up. Some old sister has recollected that just over the hill is an abandoned field (always grown up to weeds), and she thinks she would like a weed diet for a change. About five hundred others think this a pretty good idea and trail after her. The rest of the bunch prefer to keep on going in the direction in which they were headed, except three or four lame ones and a couple of old skinnies who elect to remain right where they are.

The herder wearily gets to his feet and starts after the farthest of his three bunches. Just at this critical juncture two horsemen come into sight, ride past in full view of the sheep, and go on towards the ranch. The herder knows to a moral certainty that when they get there they will tell the boss that "the sheep were split in three bunches and scattered all over hell!" With rage in his heart, and consequently with faulty judgment, the herder sends his dog when still a great distance from the farthest bunch. The dog runs about half the distance, then stops and looks around, ostensibly for further orders, but really because he would rather stand and look back than run any farther ahead. The herder motions him forward, and he runs about half the remaining distance and looks back again. This time when the herder motions him on he drops to the ground and begins to lick one of his forefeet. He does n't really have a cactus in it, but he tries his best to make the herder believe he has. However, he has not quite enough confidence in this time-worn alibi to let the herder come right up to him, for as the latter approaches with blood in his eye the dog gets up and trots on ahead, keeping just out of reach, barking brightly from time to time, trying to centre the herder's attention on the iniquities of the sheep, though knowing all the time that the blasts of lurid language assailing him from the rear are directed solely and pointedly at him. Finally, as dog and man, tandem fashion, at last approach the sheep, the dog seeks to redeem himself by a burst of speed, and quickly sends the offending sheep to join the others.

After two hours of leg work that would shame a cub reporter during a street-car strike, the herder finally manages to get his three bunches into one, and he heads them towards the distant wagon, keeping them under close and sullen guard. He arrives at the wagon at dark, with all his chores to do and supper to get before he can take any rest. Considering all the things that can and do happen to a herder in the course of his work, the wonder is not that some of them are supposed to go crazy, but that any of them stay sane.

The emperor Nero is said to have expressed the wish that the Roman people had but one head, in order that he might strike it off at a blow. Certain it is that many a herder has wished that his sheep had but one collective rear end, against which he might gratefully and repeatedly place the toe of his number eleven.

There is a certain curious experience that I have had two or three times, and I have found that other herders have had it too. I would be trying to get the sheep to do something they did n't want to do, such as crossing a stream in flood or going through a deep snowdrift, and I would be wringing wet with sweat and giving them everything I had, straining my vocal chords and vocabulary, urging on the dog, and fanning the sheep with my slicker, and right in the midst of it all some old ewe would come out of the bunch and walk up to me and smell my hand just as a dog would do, as much as to say, "You don't really mean all that, do you?" It makes a person feel particularly foolish, and he does n't know whether to laugh or to sit down and burst into tears.

The boss used to say to me sometimes, "Never get mad at the sheep. It does n't do any good. I never used to get mad when I herded." But at other times I have heard him tell how he would sometimes throw his cap on the ground and dance up and down on it and yell. Since he never got mad, it is evident that this was some form of physical culture, or perhaps his way of doing his daily dozen.

The truth is that, after you have turned the sheep back for the sixth or seventh consecutive time and they start off in a new direction with undiminished enthusiasm, there arises something within you that demands expression, just like the hot lava welling up in the bosom of an overdue volcano. The output is somewhat similar also. In fact, it would be as dangerous to hire a dumb herder, or even one with an impediment in his speech, as to construct a boiler without a safety valve. Sooner or later both would explode.

In working with horses or cattle it is possible to get at the ones who are gumming up the procession and persuade them to do differently, but it is not so with sheep. If a herder is trying unsuccessfully to drive fifteen hundred or two thousand of them somewhere that they do not want to go, obviously it is the few in front who are making all the trouble, but as the herder must stay in the rear it is impossible to get at them. He tries to instill in the rear guard such a desire for progress that they will force the leaders to go where he wishes. Often this is heart-breaking work. I remember one bunch of lambs that refused to cross a shallow stream until they had been worked with for over four hours. As they had been raised on a high divide, they had never seen running water and were afraid of it.

There are different ways of getting sheep across. The usual way is to try to push them, as described. Sometimes they can be coaxed across with grain, if there is any handy. Sometimes there is a pet sheep in the bunch that can be called across. As a last resort two or three sheep are carried across and left there to act as good examples, but only too often the good examples plunge back again as soon as they are released. To prevent this they are sometimes tied down, but in this case their struggles to get up just about counterbalance their drawing attraction.

One of the popular misconceptions about herding is that it is a monotonous job ; or, as a friend of mine put it, "Herding is all right if you don't have an active mind." But there is really little

monotony in it. The sheep rarely act the same
two days in succession. If they run one day,
they are apt to be quiet the next. They herd
differently in a high wind from what they do in a
gentle breeze. They travel with a cold wind and
against a warm one. They are apt to graze contentedly where feed is plenty and to string out
and run where the picking is poor. Herding at
one season is so different from herding at another
as almost to constitute a different job. No one
herding day is exactly like any other day, and
there is doubtless much more variety in them
than there is in the days spent in office or
factory.

One very real drawback to the herder's happiness is the constant criticism of his work by the
casual passer-by. The herder's work, more than
that of anyone else in his territory, lies open to
inspection. No one thinks of watching a farmer
at his ploughing to see whether he is drawing a
straight furrow; but as the casual rider passes a
bunch of sheep, he sizes them up for lack of
something better to do. If the sheep are scattered out, the rider decides that the herder is
careless. If they are bunched up, the herder must
be dogging them to death. If he does n't happen to see the herder, he decides that the latter
must be three miles away visiting a neighbor or

else loafing in the wagon. If he took it out in thinking, no harm would be done ; but he will inevitably pass on his theories as facts, not theories, to the next person he meets. The herder may never even hear of it, but his reputation suffers just the same. As for not seeing the herder, the latter, nine times out of ten, has seen the rider from the moment he came in sight, and will watch him out of sight. But the herder does not feel particularly called on to come down to every chance rider he sees, politely kiss his hand, and inquire after the state of his health.

The galling thing about it is that the only person competent to pass an intelligent judgment on the state of the bunch at any particular time is the one who knows how they are acting that day — namely, the herder. If the sheep are running, it is necessary to hold them up close. On the other hand, if they are quiet, it is not only possible but it is good herding to let them scatter out as they will. But perhaps it is just as well that this unjust criticism continues, because, if a herder ever learned that a passer-by had entirely approved of the way he was handling the sheep and had expressed himself to that effect, the herder would probably drop dead of excitement and surprise.

The American Federation of Labor takes

credit for the general establishment of the eight-
hour day. The United Mine Workers of America are sponsoring the five-day week. But it is
the peculiar glory of the sheepmen of the West
to have discovered the sixteen-hour day, the
seven-day week, and the thirty-one-day working month. Herding comes as near to being
a steady job as any of them. The reason, of
course, is obvious. The farm hand's work may
be picked up and dropped anywhere. If the
stockman does n't see his cattle one day, he can
see them the next — or next week, for that matter. But someone has to be with a bunch of
range sheep all day and every day, including
Sundays, Christmas, and the Fourth of July.
Consequently when the herder feels himself slipping mentally, and decides that it would be best
for all concerned that he get out of earshot of the
sheep for a while, someone must be found to take
his place, and that is not always easy. There are
always a certain number who will not under any
circumstances herd. There are others who regard
it as the old darkey did preaching: "Ah done it
once, and Ah ain't too proud to do it again."
But these broad-minded gentlemen may not be
available at the time the herder wishes to take
his lay-off. Hence it comes about that the
herder usually takes a somewhat longer vacation

once in a while, instead of resting one day a week
as the vast majority of workers do.

The herder has no use for daylight saving. He
simply can't explain it to the sheep. Consequently his working day will probably continue
to be governed by the sun, and he will leave the
Joshua-like manipulation of it to his more intelligent city brethren. The sheep usually leave the
bed ground shortly after sunrise, and they return to it sometime between sunset and dark.
The herder has few chores to do, and in that he is
more fortunate than the farm hand. It is told of
a new hand that he was kept choring around till
ten o'clock at night and then was called at four in
the morning to get a good start for the new day.
Immediately after breakfast he called for his
time. The boss asked him what the trouble was,
and received the somewhat cryptic answer, "I
never did figure to trade my bed for a lantern."

The herder does not have any troubles exactly
like this, but he does have some that the ranch
hand does n't. When the latter is through for
the day he is through, but any time of night that
the sheep may decide to leave, the herder has to
go after them and bring them back. My own belief, based on experience, is that the sheep stick
around until they see the light in the wagon go
out, and then promptly leave, knowing that the

herder will have to get up and get dressed again. It is one of their little ways of getting even. The reasons for their leaving will be mentioned later, but it is this possibility of night work that makes some sheepmen claim that a herder is hired for twenty-four hours a day. It is really only a question of time till the herder will be wearing a collar with a number on it.

Naturally, there is always the temptation to cut a little off the working day; I mean temptation for the herder, of course. This does not necessarily mean that the sheep would be cut short on their grazing time, but that the herder would leave the wagon as late as possible and return to it as early as he considered safe. But there is always more or less of a sporting chance to this, and many a herder has wandered around a little when he first got out in the morning, praying that he might find his sheep before the boss found them, or him. It was probably some such accident that lay behind the story of the herder who suddenly presented himself before the boss at the ranch buildings one morning and asked if he wished to have him keep on herding. "Why, yes!" said the surprised boss. "I have no kick on your work." "All right, then," said the relieved herder, "you'd better give me another bunch of sheep. I lost those."

IV

THE HERDER'S PARTNERS

"Ten thousand white ones and sixty black ones ! Go round 'em, Shep !" This command was supposed to have been given to a certain sheep dog in Montana, and presumably he thereupon rounded up the sheep and counted them. But the poor dog is dead now; brain fever, no doubt. It is strange that when anyone tells a tale of some extraordinary animal, be it dog, horse, or cat, he usually adds as an afterthought, "He's dead now, poor fellow." In fact, someone with time to spare ought to make a study of the high mortality rate among canine and other animal wonders; and after satisfying himself on that point he might turn to a closely allied topic, the regrettable longevity of cheerful liars.

It is said that in some parts of the West there is a set price for a trained sheep dog, about forty dollars. Such a dog would be one taught to work entirely by motions, to go to the right or left, to stop and lie down, and to return. If a wind is blowing against the herder, it is impossible for him to make the dog hear at any great distance, but he can direct him by motions as far as the dog can see him. Of course it takes good dog material to make a first-class sheep dog, as well as a good man to train him. However, in our part of the country we use any kind of dog that will turn the sheep, and then do as they do in Kansas, where they do the best they can. Naturally collies predominate, for they seem to take to sheep and herding by instinct.

Instinct, however, will not tell any dog the various things he must not do. A pup always wants to work too fast. When he starts going around a bunch of sheep, he gets so excited and is having such a good time that he forgets to pay attention to the herder, and often goes completely around the bunch, sometimes two or three times. Of course this ties the sheep up in a knot, causes them unnecessary worry and alarm, and delays their grazing. Often, too, the pup will cut off a little bunch of sheep and drive them away from the main band. This makes serious trouble for the herder, who may have to walk half a mile after them, and naturally he makes trouble for the dog. Perhaps the commonest fault a pup has is cutting off a single sheep and trying to run it down, keeping between it and the rest of the bunch. This herding of one sheep instead of fifteen hundred is looked on by the herder with strong disfavor. Gradually, after being punished for one thing and another, the dog learns what he must and must not do and becomes the herder's indispensable ally.

Of course, it is just as easy to ruin a dog in the training as it is to spoil a horse or a child. Though without any first-hand knowledge of the last-named process, it is my belief that all three rest on much the same principles. They all call for firmness, for kindness, for genuine affection, and above all for infinite patience.

One of the worst habits a dog can form is rabbit chasing. The bunch may be scattered out peacefully grazing, when the dog scents a rabbit somewhere up the wind. He goes to investigate ; the rabbit jumps up, and the chase is on. The rabbit will always go uphill if he can, because on account of his short front legs he is a better hill climber than the dog. He may or may not go through the sheep ; he has no prejudice against so doing. If he does go through them, followed of course by the dog, it means that they will bunch up, lose valuable grazing time, and perhaps start running. Besides this, the dog will tire himself out and get sore feet by habitual rabbit running, and then when the herder has to call on him for help he is often unable or unwilling to give it.

One dog is all a herder needs, but the dog seems to enjoy life more if he has a companion. He eats better, and he has an opportunity to play and romp, which a dog likes so well. But if a herder has more than two dogs, he might as well go somewhere and get a job as pound master, where he will get paid for taking care of dogs. If he has three dogs, one or two of them will be misbehaving in some way all the time, and the herder will find that he is taking care of dogs instead of sheep. It is the application of the old saying, "One boy's a boy, two boys half a boy, three boys no boy." Then there is the serious problem of feeding them. A herder can always scrape up enough for one dog, but three dogs will eat twice as much as the herder himself.

A dog is the one thing of which sheep are afraid. They move merely enough to keep out of a herder's way, and they care nothing about a horse, in case the herder happens to be riding. Many a sheep's leg has been broken by a horse stepping on it. But a dog is a horse of another color. The sheep have the same respect for him that a small boy has for a policeman, and about the same liking. They can tell a strange dog as far as they can see him. They are always curious about a new dog, and when one is around you can see every sheep on the edge of the bunch sizing him up. They come as close to him as they dare, to investigate. But they move for him when he is on business.

There is, however, a great difference in the way sheep react to different dogs after they know them. From a fast-working dog they run in terror, while for a slow dog, usually an old one, they move with corresponding leisure. The ideal dog is one that works slowly but steadily, looking back frequently for further directions from the herder.

There is no doubt that a dog, especially a young one, enjoys herding, for any dog likes to chase something that will run. There are, however, only two motives that will keep a dog working — namely, love of the work, and liking for the herder. Fear of the herder will not influence him, because while he is working he is out of the herder's reach ; and a dog that is abused will quit the herder altogether and go to the ranch.

While the dog is the herder's ever-present companion, there are two occasions on which he

sticketh closer than a brother. If the herder is
climbing a slippery bank and taking each step
with extreme care, the dog invariably senses this
as a good opportunity to demonstrate the affection that has been piling up within him. He
gets in front of the herder, about on a level with
the latter's face, and unless he is warned off he
will put his paws on the herder's shoulders and
roll him to the bottom. And if the herder happens to be crossing new and thin ice where an
additional pound or two may cause him to break
through and give him wet feet for the rest of the
day, the faithful dog will stick close at his heels
and no amount of low-voiced cursing can drive
him away.

A young dog just starting in always wants to
work fast. As a rule, the older a dog grows, the
slower he gets. The novelty of the work wears
off, and from being a kind of play it becomes a
grind. Finally, the dog seems to arrive at the
somewhat anarchistic conclusion that the world
owes him a living whether he works or not.
Usually by this time his services have earned him
a long vacation, and he is retired on full pay —
that is, a full stomach — for the rest of his days.

It is not necessary to remind those who have
had to do with dogs that even members of the
same breed have strong individualities, one

might almost say personalities. I have used a dozen dogs in the last ten years, and no one of them even remotely resembled the others in disposition. One would be fast, another slow; one lazy, and another eager. The first dog I used was a fuzzy nondescript named Jack. He never really became a sheep dog, and whatever he did was done out of affection for the herder. He was rough with the sheep and tore several of them in his time. He had an absolutely incurable habit of barking, one of the most annoying faults a sheep dog can have. In fact, he had about every bad habit there is, except rabbit chasing, and he was too lazy for that. But he had one quality that counterbalanced all his failings, and that was his single-minded devotion. I called him everything that the English language permitted, and even stretched a point or two upon occasion, and yet I could n't bear the thought of parting with him permanently. He made so much trouble around the sheep that I used to leave him at the ranch when the wagon was moved. He would be satisfied there for a day or two, and then would return to the bed ground where the wagon was stationed last. Not finding it there, he would go back to the ranch, and the next day would scout around in a new direction. Of course he knew all the bed grounds that we used, and he would make the rounds of them until he found the sheep, the wagon, and the herder. And then he would do everything but talk. Much had to be forgiven a devotion like that.

Then there was Noka, as pretty as a dog could be. I used to think that she consciously posed, and she might well have been forgiven for doing so. She was a spotted dog of the breed called Mexican shepherd. She was just getting into her stride when she mysteriously disappeared.

Then there was Laddie, poor loving faithful Laddie, who crowded more suffering into his eighteen months of life than most dogs would into a long stretch of years. I was gone on a Christmas vacation and the sheep were at the ranch, but Laddie, who was only a pup then, somehow got the idea that I was in the wagon or that I should return to it. So for three days and three nights he lay on the snow beside the wagon tongue, while the thermometer rose in the daytime and sunk at night, but never during those three days rose above zero. What Laddie suffered can only be imagined. Four months later, not twenty rods from where he had endured the tortures of cold, he picked up a poison bait intended for a coyote, and he died with all the fires of hell gnawing at his vitals. The age-old problems of unmerited pain and suffering are not confined to the human race.

The dog I am using at present is an inveterate rabbit chaser. I had always thought that his ambition was nothing less than the extermination of the entire rabbit species, but something that happened a short time ago shook my faith in this theory. We surprised a big jack rabbit in the feed yard, which is surrounded by woven wire. Bobbie immediately made a rush for the rabbit, and the rabbit for the fence, where he got stuck halfway through the fine mesh and lay kicking and struggling. Bobbie was right at his heels, but instead of making rabbit meat of him, as I expected, he merely danced all around him in a high state of excitement, watching him, until I half expected to see Bobbie raise one paw and push the rabbit on through. I found out right then that Bobbie did n't want to catch rabbits; all he wanted to do was to chase them, like the man who followed the bear tracks all day and then quit them because they were getting too fresh.

A dog is supposed to be one of the most intelligent of animals, and yet a pack of hounds will tackle a porcupine and come home with their jaws looking as if they had chewed a pincushion, will suffer all kinds of torment while the barbed quills are pulled out or pushed through, and then the next day perhaps will go out and get another mouthful of the same. But to the sheep dog's credit be it said that he is not nearly so likely to get into this kind of mess as is the hound.

Considering the indispensable help that a dog renders a herder, it is not strange that between the two there exists an unusually close bond. Certainly there is a feeling that could not be comprehended by the proprietor of some three-and-a-half-pound mixture of long hair and bad temper masquerading under the name of dog; because the affection existing between a herder and his dog rests on the solid basis of mutual respect. Moreover, the dog is the herder's sole companion during most of the time, because the sheep cannot by any stretch of the imagination be termed good company. They are too intent on their own affairs. The dog, however, is the herder's ever-present friend. He stays by his side during the day and sleeps in the wagon at night; and when the herder is without his dog for a day or so, he misses this companionship quite as much as he does the dog's aid.

One evening when I came to my wagon, I found on the table a note from a neighboring herder, asking me to come over to his wagon, about half a mile away. I went over immediately, and found that both of his dogs had died that afternoon from picking up poison baits put out for coyotes. The herder had not known the location of the poison. He was about half a mile from the wagon when the dogs were taken sick, and he started for it immediately to do what he could for them. He carried the pup in his arms, and when he arrived he gave both dogs salt and water as an emetic, followed by warm lard as an antidote. But he could not save them. The young dog, having less resistance, died first. Then the herder had to go out after his sheep, as it was getting dark. The old dog, in spite of all the herder could do, insisted on going with him. The herder was a middle-aged man, and hard-boiled at that, but his face was working as he told me how the old dog would struggle after him through the deep snow, how he would fall down in convulsions, then rise and drag himself on again, until that final convulsion from which he did not rise. As the herder finished he went to the door of his wagon and looked out at the falling snow. "Well," he said, "the snow will cover them and they will rest forever." I knew what he felt, because two of my own dogs were sleeping that same sleep, fallen soldiers in the grim and unrelenting war against the killers of the sheep.

"More good herders have been ruined by a horse than by any other one thing." This is the lament of some who see a sign of the degeneracy of the times in the fact that many herders do their stuff nowadays astride a horse. But modern pessimists who take as their model of perfection the days of the stagecoach and the tallow dip are always with us ; and if, or rather when, our reformers shall have made the manufacture and sale of eating tobacco a capital offense, there will probably be some who will mourn the passing of the old decorated shirt bosom with its plain or fancy pattern etched in tobacco juice, which doubtless was aimed right, but fell far short of its mark.

The arguments against a horse for the herder seem to be twofold. In the first place, there is the idea that if the herder is afoot he will spend his time walking briskly from point to point, on the *qui vive* and tirelessly vigilant. The truth is, of course, that he won't. He won't walk, or ride, any farther than is necessary to keep the bunch in good order. Furthermore, nobody is on the *qui vive* fourteen hours a day, except the hero of an Alger book, and he is either dead or wealthy by this time. Of course the herder is reasonably vigilant, but if by that you picture him sitting on a hill and rolling his eyes ceaselessly over and around the sheep, you will have him counting his fingers before the week is out.

The other reason alleged against the use of a horse is based on the supposition that herding is a lazy man's job, "nothing to do, and all day to do it in." This theory is held chiefly by those who have n't tried it, and particularly by those who are themselves too lazy ever to give it a trial. The reasoning then runs something like this: herding being a lazy man's job, and the herder therefore lazy, if he is allowed to ride a horse instead of walking he will become still lazier, and will inevitably be attacked by pernicious anæmia, bed boils, or some such kindred menace. Old Alec Connell, Roosevelt's Harding County friend, used to say that he always dreaded returning to the ranch after a prolonged absence, for fear he might find the hired man starved to death in bed. The best corrective of this hallucination as regards herding would be to have the theorist chaperon the sheep some day when they have the spirit of travel in their feet. His repudiation of his theory would be complete, final, and sincere.

There is no good reason, aside from a respect for tradition, why the herder should not use a horse in summer, and most of them now do. There are practical reasons in favor of it. If the sheep are quiet, the farther they spread out the better for them. But after the bunch gets too far extended, the herder loses control if he is afoot, it being impossible for him to get the sheep together within a reasonable time. But with a horse to aid him, he can let the sheep do pretty much as they please and still keep control of them. A horse does not in any way take the place of a dog, but simply enables herder and dog to arrive more quickly at any desired point.

This does not apply to winter herding. No one with any regard for a horse would think of putting him on a picket rope in winter. The days are too short and the nights too long for any such arrangement, and there is too little protection from the cold. A horse might be staked in a sheltered spot in the evening, but a change of wind during the night would expose him to suffering. It is no hardship for a loose horse to be out, for he can always hunt up a sheltered spot ; but a picketed horse is defenseless. Therefore, from the time the nights turn cold in the fall until green grass comes in the spring, the herder goes afoot. This is not such a hardship as it might seem, for when snow is on the ground the sheep do not travel nearly so far as when it is bare.

The requirements for a herder's horse are very different from those of a cowboy's. The ideal herding horse has only one interest in life, and that one is eating. The more nearly devoid of other ideas he is, the better for the herder. Especially should he have a blank and incurious mind with regard to any other horses he may see. The trouble is that the range horses will not be indifferent to him, but will come up and try to get acquainted. To them the ideal herding horse will pay no attention whatsoever, but will single-mindedly go on trying to push his skin as far as possible from his ribs.

Once in a while you will find a horse that can be turned loose near the wagon at night and be found somewhere in the neighborhood of the wagon in the morning; but such horses are rare. The herder is well satisfied if his horse will graze close by him during the day under saddle, and at night he will picket him in a bunch of good grass or hobble him out. In either case the horse can get plenty to eat, and his work is not hard. Of course a herder can ride a horse down doing unnecessary work, just as he can work a dog sore-footed in a single day. But there is no need of doing either.

The herder's real trouble comes when he has a horse that will not stand without being held or tied, and such horses are numerous. Since the horse must graze during the day as well as at night, the only thing for the herder to do is to take a picket rope with him and keep hold of one end of it, if there is no convenient sagebush to tie it to. This gets monotonous, and the herder gets to trusting the horse a little, or forgets and lets the rope out of his hand, and the next minute he is gazing after the rapidly receding form of his horse. It is a case where distance lends no enchantment.

Buffalo Bill in his autobiography tells how he walked thirty-five miles behind a government mule, which kept just far enough ahead to keep from being caught. He shot the mule just before he reached the fort for which they were both headed. Many a herder can appreciate the great scout's feelings on that occasion, although he may not be able to satisfy his own as completely as Buffalo Bill did. You walk after the horse, thinking all the while that you will give him the ride of his life on the way back, and that you will do this, that, and the other thing to him. Finally you get him in a fence corner, or he decides to let you catch him, and when the moment of capture arrives you realize that if you act as your feelings prompt you to do he will be just that much harder to catch the next time, and that you may be exchanging a doubtful present gratification for a very certain amount of future grief, for the horse is bound to get loose again sooner or later. As you ride him back, in the pleasure of being able to escape walking, your feelings towards him change and soften. You decide not to make any reprisals whatever, and peace reënters and possesses your soul.

Horses, however, like people, sometimes change their dispositions. I have a chestnut mare named Bess, who used to be a model sheep horse. She had a vast indifference as regarded other equines, and would graze contentedly within a quarter of a mile of a bunch of range horses without so much as raising her head. Then she had a colt and ran out for a year, and she was never the same after that. Now, in her old age, she forgets the dignity that should characterize a great-grandmother. It is possible that she has heard about the new freedom of woman. At any rate, she takes a lively interest in any bunch of horses she sees, makes a regular practice of speaking to utter strangers, and declares herself in on every equine gathering. She has become nothing less than a social gadabout, and her late-blooming giddiness has just about ruined her for a herding horse. Other times, other manners. I expect she will be bobbing her mane and tail next.

V

THE YEARLY ROUND

IT has always been hard for me to understand why the big city newspapers publish daily weather reports and forecasts, for the city dweller can have only an academic interest in the weather at best. In the morning he leaves a warm, comfortable house, walks a block or two in whatever weather happens to exist, enters a street car or "L," and is carried to the door of his place of business. In the evening he reverses the process, braving the weather for perhaps ten minutes before reaching the shelter of home. It may well be that the paper publishes an account of the weather simply as news, because the city man might never notice what the weather was unless it were called to his attention in this way. The proof of this is that the city man wears much the same clothing the year round. He could wear a straw hat at all seasons as far as physical comfort goes. Thousands of him go through the winter snugly encased in B. V. D.'s. Of course it would be idle for a herder to speculate on what the ladies wear, and immoral to speculate as to why, but from the Sunday supplements and magazine illustrations, his only sources of information, it would seem that the ladies are animated, winter and summer, by that spirit of drastic economy that leads them to keep their clothing as near the vanishing point as liberal police regulations will allow.

The country dweller, however, being more a child of Nature, is more attentive to her moods. The farmer's interest in the weather is proverbial; that of the farm hand is still more intense and personal; but the sheep herder's interest in it eclipses them all. For him the weather is not an academic subject, but the most practical subject there is. It governs the actions of the sheep and his own comfort. It dictates his food and his clothing. In midsummer he may go modestly clad in shoes, shirt, and overalls. In winter he is still more modestly clad in two pairs of trousers and a heavy sweater, to say nothing of a sheep coat. From sunrise to sunset, every day in the year, he must take the weather, whatever it may be.

In fact the weather is such an all important factor in a herder's life that herding through the four seasons of the year is almost like holding four different jobs in succession. Of course they shade into each other by imperceptible gradations, as day passes into night, but in their essence they differ almost as much as day and night. Some herders prefer one season, some another; but by unanimous consent the worst season of all is the verdant springtime.

Countless poets have expressed the emotions aroused in them by the sight of Nature putting on her mantle of green again. Countless herders have done the same. But here the resemblance ceases, for while the poet may find a publisher willing to preserve his thoughts on the annual rejuvenation of the grass, the no less sincere outpourings of the herder on the same subject are all unprintable. From a herder's standpoint the green grass is the villain of the piece. Imagine a child, particularly fond of candy, who has been deprived of it for six months or so, and then picture him turned loose in a candy shop and told to help himself. You can easily figure out how much control you would have over him for the next half hour. After he had had his fill, he would be amenable to reason again. This is precisely what happens to the sheep. They have been on dry feed all winter, whether hay or grass cured on the ground, and then, with the coming of spring, they get the chance to eat tender green grass once more. No wonder they go wild. But the trouble is that the grass comes gradually, its growth still further retarded by cold spells and late frosts. The sheep, however, smell the green before it is fairly above the ground, and they run everywhere searching for a place where it is plentiful, naturally without finding it. Even when the grass is an inch or two high, it seems impossible for them to get their fill of it. They crop a mouthful here, run a few steps, grab another mouthful, and run a few steps more. They always seem to think that the grass is plentiful just beyond them, and they lose no time in getting there. Ordinarily a ewe will graze first on one side of her, then on the other, and then move forward a step ; but when hunger for green grass drives her on, she will take four or five steps between each two bites. That carries the bunch forward at an unusual rate. The period of running lasts until green grass is so plentiful that the sheep can get their fill of it every day, the length of the period depending on how fast the grass grows and how many setbacks it has, which in turn depends wholly and exclusively on the weather.

If anyone thinks that a sheep can't run, just let him try to head one off. When "running" in spring, the entire bunch moves faster than the herder can walk. One herder told me of an experience he said he had with a bunch of antelope. His sheep passed them on the run, so just for an experiment he threw the antelope into the bunch as they loped past. The antelope kept up for a while, but the pace told on them and soon they were in distress. Their sides were heaving, their flanks dripped with sweat, and their tongues lolled out till they were in danger of being stepped on. Finally, the herder said, he was unable to stand the sight of their suffering any longer, so he cut them back and left them to throw themselves on the ground and recuperate. Like the rest of us, he had always believed that the antelope were the fastest things on the plains, but now, he said, he knew better. I do not vouch for the truth of this story, merely giving it as it was told to me. But there can be little doubt that many a jack rabbit has been trampled to death through sheer inability to keep ahead of some old ewe looking for green grass. I have often thought that it might be a profitable experiment to enter a bunch of sheep on the race tracks of the East. There are only two objections that I can think of : one is that perhaps nobody would want to bet on a sheep, and the other, that the present title holders would all have to get other jobs, such as pulling ploughs and horse cars.

It is not only the running, however, that makes sheep difficult to handle in the spring, but the fact that they spread out so quickly. At ordinary times, sheep have a very strong herd instinct. A small boy was asked by his teacher how many, out of five sheep in a field, would be left if one jumped over the fence. He answered correctly, "None." "Why, Johnny," remonstrated the teacher, "one from five leaves four." "Well," replied Johnny, "you may know arithmetic, but you don't know sheep." Of course it is only this strong herd instinct that makes it possible for two or three thousand sheep to be handled by one man. In fact, certain breeds of sheep that do not have this instinct so strongly cannot be run on the open range at all, but must be kept in woven-wire pastures. However, when the green grass is coming, even the close-herd-

ing sheep seem to throw off their inhibitions
temporarily, and it seems as if every ewe, for-
getting the rest of the bunch, grazes straight
out in front of her. The sheep spread out much
faster than the herder can throw them together.
Of course the dog can turn them, but even he
has his limits and can be used only so much.
It usually takes the assistance of a saddle horse
in addition to keep the whole bunch in one
county.

Besides the running, splitting, and spreading
in spring, there are other factors that induce in
the herder the belief that he has mistaken his
vocation. The frost has come out of the ground,
creek bottoms are soft, every low place is muddy,
and some of them are boggy. The sheep are in
the poorest physical condition of the entire year.
They have stood the strain of the winter's cold,
the green grass has weakened them temporarily,
they are heavy with lamb, and the muddy going
is the proverbial last straw. Sheep get bogged
down in muddy spots and wait patiently for
death or the herder. They try to cross streams
in deep places, their wool takes up water like a
sponge, and they are unable to climb out on the
other side. The really weak sheep will run
themselves ragged when headed away from the
wagon, and then, when they are turned towards

it, they simply drop from exhaustion. It is no uncommon thing to find the weakest ewe in the bunch at the very tip of the lead, and quite often she finds that she has lost her return ticket.

In fact one of the peculiar things about sheep is the extraordinary facility with which they take leave of life, and the great variety of ways in which they make their exits. You might almost accuse them of having a morbid strain. It so happens that several methods of dying are in vogue during the spring months, and often the heaviest loss of the year occurs at this time. When the snow first softens, the draws or swales are filled with slush, which may have the appearance of snow; but when a ewe tries to cross it, she finds herself in a medium where she can neither swim nor struggle through. I have seen four sheep drowned in slush within twenty feet of each other. They also get stuck in soft creek bottoms and either drown or chill to death. A weak ewe may be unable to make it back to the wagon, and the herder will throw the sheep that way next day to pick her up, only to find her missing or killed by coyotes. With the sheep running as they do at this time, a small bunch may cut off unseen by the herder and lose some of its number by coyotes before the remainder are picked up. At any time a coyote may sneak up a draw and kill a ewe before his presence is discovered. In addition there are certain weeds that are deadly poison to sheep, and even wet grass after a rain may occasionally bloat one. Sometimes a number may be killed by licking too much alkali along the creeks. Besides this they are subject to all the diseases of the organs, as other creatures are, with a few peculiar to themselves thrown in for good measure.

The most peculiar method of all is that called "dying on their backs." When horses or dogs roll, they either roll all the way over or roll back to the position from which they started; they are unable to balance themselves on their spine, as it were. But when a sheep rolls and reaches a position with its legs pointing upwards, it is often unable to complete the turn, especially if it has a heavy coat of wool, as is the case in spring. The reason for this is that a sheep's legs, being very thin, are not able to exert any pull to one side or the other and thus aid the sheep in righting itself. A horse's legs, being long and heavy, can exert a powerful leverage on his body and turn it, but when a sheep is on its back, its centre of gravity lies wholly within it, and there is no leverage it can bring to bear. Its only chance is to twist itself violently, in the hope that some movement may turn it on its side. If unsuccessful in this, the unnatural position for some reason causes gas to collect in its body, and it begins to bloat. Finally the pressure of this gas on its heart and lungs becomes so terrific that these organs cease to function. If the ewe is found at any time before life is extinct and is turned over on her stomach, she will get up, stagger off, and deflate, looking meanwhile like a misshapen balloon. There is a great variation in the time it takes a sheep to die on her back. She may be dead in fifteen minutes, then again she may be alive at the end of an hour or more ; it all depends on how full her stomach was to start with. But die she will, unless discovered and turned right side up. Sheep are especially apt to roll when the sun comes out warm after a rain. The herder may turn over half a dozen sheep in a day, when conditions are such as to make them roll, and he has to be eternally on the lookout for them. The price of their lives is his vigilance.

Finally, to fill the herder's cup of woe to overflowing, the days in spring are interminably long. They approach in length the farmer's eight-hour day — eight hours before dinner and eight hours after. This has one single advantage. It gives the herder time mentally to reshape his future life, so that he will never under any circumstances have to herd through another spring.

At the latter end of spring comes lambing, and after that shearing, but these are such important events in the sheep herder's calendar that they must be given a separate chapter. Continuing now with the herding year, we come to summer, a season differing radically from the other three as regards herding. All the rest of the year the herder leaves the wagon in the morning carrying a lunch, and does not return to it until evening. His evening meal is apt to be the principal one of the day, and he does most of his cooking then. But in summer every day is really broken into two working days. The reason for this is that the sheep will not graze during the intense heat of a summer's midday, but will run to the nearest water and lie beside it till late in the afternoon. Consequently in summer the wagon is placed beside a stream or water hole, and the day's schedule is somewhat as follows : —

The sheep leave the bed ground about five o'clock, or shortly after sunrise, and go out to graze, usually working against the wind. The herder snatches a hasty breakfast and overtakes them with the aid of his saddle horse. The band grazes until the sun gets uncomfortably hot, and then some of the sheep start for water. They do not all go at once, but fall gradually into long lines. Usually they follow deep dusty paths already made by thirsty stock, and the long lines of sheep smoking down to water on a hot summer's day are as characteristic of a sheep country as the sheep themselves. A certain professor, although brought up on a farm, hazarded the opinion that sheep never drink, which merely shows that even a college professor should stick closely to his own subject.

When the sheep reach water, they drink, and then huddle together in large groups, usually with their heads beneath one another's sides. That is, as you look at the bunch you can see only their backs, their heads being down near the cool wet sand, where there is protection also from the mosquitoes and flies. A few may lie down, but most of them stand huddled together right at the water's edge. Occasionally a lamb or two may stand in the water for the sake of coolness, but a grown sheep almost never. If there are any banks close by to cast a shadow, this patch of shade will be packed as full of sheep as it can hold.

The sheep will probably all be on water by eleven o'clock, and from then on till three or four in the afternoon the herder is free to do as he pleases. This does not mean that he can make a practice of visiting away from the wagon, because there is always the chance that a stray coyote may drop in for dinner. But since the wagon overlooks the sheep as they lie on water, the herder has four or five hours in which to cook, eat dinner, read, write, or otherwise recreate himself.

About three or four o'clock the sheep begin to leave water. They straggle off one by one grazing into the wind, and it will perhaps be an hour before the last one leaves. The herder does not have to follow until they are pretty well out, and occasionally he does not have to leave the wagon in the afternoon at all. The sheep do not travel as fast or as far as they do in the morning, and their grazing time is shorter. They reach the bed ground about dark, the herder going in ahead of them to prepare his evening meal.

The result of this schedule is that the noon meal becomes the principal one of the day, because there is then plenty of time to cook, while there is little time to spare for either of the other meals. This is a pity, because it forces the herder to hover over his stove during the hottest part of the day and to convert his wagon into a little inferno. But even at that, the heat of a Dakota sun at noon is such as to tempt the herder to crawl into his oven to cool off — like the Arizona man being cremated in Chicago, who, after spending an hour in the furnace, sat up in his coffin and cursed the attendant for opening the door and letting in a draft. It takes an inland country like the Great Northwest or Siberia to produce extremes of heat and cold.

As stated before, the wagon without a fire in it is very comfortable even on a hot day, since it is open at both ends. It does not take a wood fire long to die down, and as soon as the stove cools off the herder is as comfortable as may be. Since he does not have to leave the wagon till the cool of the day approaches, he really does not suffer with the heat, and does not have to stand nearly so much of it as the farm hand does. Often he prepares a cold supper to avoid heating up the wagon again before he goes to bed. Summer herding, then, means early rising and consequently early retiring, but it provides several hours of freedom in the middle of the day.

There are times in the year, notably in spring, when the herder may envy the ranch hand, but as the herder lies on his bed through the heat of a summer's day and through the open door of the wagon watches the distant ranch hand sweating up and down the corn rows, or pitching hay, or doing some other work that requires a strong back and a weak mind, he is apt to be pharisaically thankful that he is not as one of these.

One real drawback to summer is the flies.

They are not bad at first, but from the beginning of August they become a pest and a torment. Since the door and the window of the wagon both open out, it is impossible to screen against them. The only way is to fight them as they come in. I have killed, by actual count, six hundred flies with a swatter in one afternoon. I might add that I did little else during that time. The best way seems to be to let them accumulate for a day or two and then shut the wagon up and give them a dose of some good insecticide. That wipes the slate clean and gives a chance for a fresh start. But even at that, is n't it a wonder that Pharaoh did n't let the Israelites go immediately after the plague of flies? He must have been a glutton for punishment.

Time and tide, they say, wait for no man. Gradually the days become shorter, the heat moderates, and the sheep lie on water a shorter time each day. The first really cool day they do not stop on water at all, but merely drink and go on ; or perhaps they do not go down to water at all. And about this time, as summer is slipping into fall, comes "shipping." The bunch is taken in to the ranch. The wether lambs, that is, the males, are first cut out and penned by themselves. Then all the ewes that show signs of age are cut out and put in a separate pen. The sheepman then examines the mouths of these old ones to see which have teeth enough to carry them through another winter. The "gummers," that is, those that have lost all their teeth, and the "broken mouths," those that have some teeth missing, are cut out and put in with the wethers, and the rest are returned to the bunch. A sheep's age can be accurately told by the number and state of its teeth. A yearling has two teeth, a two-year-old four, a three-year-old six, and a four-year-old eight, or a full mouth, as it is called. At five a ewe's teeth are apt to begin to spread and to be worn down. From then on, individuals differ somewhat, some losing their teeth quickly and some keeping them for a year or two longer. Ordinarily, it does not pay a man who runs sheep on the range to keep his ewes after their mouths begin to break. They will be all right for a year or two, where they have plenty of hay and some grain, but range conditions are too hard for them. Consequently the sheepman culls out his gummers and broken mouths each fall at the time he markets his lambs, and thus gets his bunch in shape for the coming winter.

Then begins the journey to the railroad with the lambs, and often the regular herder makes the trip for the sake of a change. From the region where we are it is fifty-five miles to the

railroad on the north and seventy-five miles if we
go south.   The longer route entails in addition
the crossing of a gumbo belt thirty miles wide.
Now gumbo, when it is dry, is a black powdery
soil, crisscrossed by innumerable tiny lines, like
the wrinkles in the face of a very old man ;
when it is wet, it forms a sea of black mud of un-
believable viscosity.   When the gumbo is dry,
the roads crossing it are like boulevards paved
with asphalt ; but when it is wet, these same
roads are indescribable.   Suffice to say that in
wet weather the very chickens get stuck, that
when any vehicle goes along the road it ploughs
great ruts as the gumbo clings affectionately to
the wheels until scraped off by some more gumbo
that wants to get on and ride.   They say down
there that you don't leave the road, you take it
with you.   I heard a man declare that he once
got stuck with six ponies on a buckboard going
downhill, but I never knew whether to believe
him or not.   Certain it is that if you walk there
after a rain you will be surprised at the increasing weight of your feet, and if you look behind
at your tracks you will think somebody has been
digging a row of post holes.   You will also notice
the inhabitants going around prying their chickens loose, and laying them on their backs so that
the mud on their feet will dry.   A little later,

after the ground has dried and hardened, you will notice them blasting the earth loose around the feet of the horse and cow, so that they can move around and graze once more. When Henry Ford gets into his promised quantity production of flivver planes, the gumbo farmer will be enabled to crank up and fly down to his barn to do chores no matter what the weather is, instead of waiting for a dry spell as he has to do at present. If anyone ever discovers what gumbo was really made for, all the glue factories will have to close. The consequence of all this is that when distances are about equal most people prefer to move their stock over the sand, where it can navigate in all weathers.

The trip to the railroad takes from six to eight days. It is always an interesting event, even though it is harder than the herder's regular work. Often two or three sheepmen throw in together; and as the lambs are all freshly branded when they start, they can be easily sorted out at the shipping point.

If there are even a few old ewes in the bunch, it is not difficult to get the band "trail-broke"; but if it is a straight bunch of lambs, the first few days are lively ones. Someone has said that "a ewe has just sense enough to be ornery." But a lamb does n't know even that much. A band of ewes will keep a certain direction without much bother, but direction means less than nothing to a lamb. A rabbit, a Russian thistle, or any little thing at all is sufficient to change his previous intentions, if any. He is afraid of running water and of everything else but a fence. He is always glad to see a fence and always suspects that there is a ripe grain field on the other side of it, and he is a great one to act on his suspicions. But by degrees he steadies down, learns to keep direction fairly well, and by the time he reaches the railroad he is as easy to handle as a ewe would be at the start.

Two men go with each bunch of lambs on the trail. One drives the lambs, and the other the wagon or truck that carries the camp outfit. The second man also makes and breaks camp, does the cooking and dish washing, and helps the other fellow at a pinch. It is right here that the chance for trouble comes in. It is natural for the one driving the sheep to want all the help he can get, and it is just as natural for the other to fail to recognize the "pinch" when it arrives. Each is apt to think that the other is putting the burden on him, and it is a tradition that of the dozens of pairs of men who start with the lambs few arrive at the railroad on the same cordial terms with which they started.

But with good weather the trip can be a very pleasant one.   Old friendships are renewed along the road and new ones made.   There are sheep ahead and behind, and there is visiting back and forth among the trailsmen.   There is always the discussion of what happened at this or that point last year.   There is news of the progress of the other bands in line, news spread by trucks or cars that traverse the whole route every day on their way to and from the railroad.   Finally there is the sight of a real town and of the railroad once more, the crowded stock pens, the dusty job of "cutting" the bunch again and again as each man's sheep are sorted from the rest, the crowding of the sheep on to the scales, the cutting into carload lots, and the prodding of the sheep up the runways into the double-decked cars.   Then comes the ride up to the hotel, the removal of at least a portion of the corral dust, the good dinner on clean tables served by pretty waitresses (they all look pretty after a summer spent in the exclusive society of the sheep), and the time spent lounging around town afterward.   Last of all there is the trip home, covering in hours the route that took days on the up trip ; then back to the wagon and the sheep again.

While the herder is escorting his erstwhile charges on the first lap of their last journey, the

depressing thought is apt to come to him that almost all the animal life on a ranch is destined for
the shambles. The male lambs never live their
first year out, and their sisters follow them as
soon as age has unfitted them for the range.
According to this view of things, the ranch becomes an incipient charnel house, and the herder
and the ranch hand are assistants to the undertaker. But a little further thought brings the
reflection that death is in any case inevitable and
inescapable, and that the herder is headed for it
just as surely as the lamb who is even now singing
down the rails on his way to market. The main
difference between them is that there is no present market for herder meat. Herder on the
hoof is still in demand, but a dead herder is a
total loss.

It becomes, then, a question of the kind of
death the lamb shall meet, and in this respect
there can be no regret for his charges on the part
of the herder. Those who are in a position to
know tell us that the life of every wild thing ends
in a tragedy. Surely the swift and merciful
death of the slaughterhouse is infinitely preferable to cruel death at the jaws of the coyote, or
slow death from starvation, exposure, or disease.
The whole question becomes one of euthanasia ;
and while there may be arguments on both sides

as to the application of this principle to the human race, there can scarcely be any when it is applied to the animal kingdom.

Moreover, in the case of the old ewes, the butcher confers an added benefit on them, in that after death they attain a rejuvenation which would be impossible for them in this life. For the toothless gummer, having lived to a ripe old age, having seen her children's children, and having closed her eyes peacefully if somewhat hastily on this world, makes one final appearance on the dinner table, decorated with parsley and with her youth renewed under the title of "lamb."

Restored to his range, the herder enters on the golden season of the herding year, the autumn. This is the rose without a thorn. The days are reasonably short and growing shorter, and the herder once more has an evening that is worthy of the name. The weather is neither too hot nor too cold for comfort. The sheep have an abundance of feed and graze contentedly. Flies have disappeared, and the herder no longer has to strain his coffee through his teeth. Truly, it is a solemn thought to be the mausoleum of unnumbered flies. The bunch of sheep is smaller than it has been for several months, with half the lambs gone and a hundred or so of the old sheep, and therefore it is easier to handle.

Everything seems to conspire to make herding the most enjoyable job in the world.   And yet on the horizon is a little cloud, no larger than a man's hand, and that cloud is the thought of the approaching winter.

VI

BLAST AND BLIZZARD

There was a young man of Quebec,
Who was buried in snow to the neck;
 When they asked, "Are you friz?"
 He replied, "Yes, I is;
But we don't call that cold in Quebec."

WE don't call it cold in South Dakota, either.
But when the mercury sinks until it drops out of
the bottom of the thermometer and rolls around
on the floor, and then freezes up so that the baby
can play marbles with it, that's cold!

There is locally, however, a difference of opinion regarding South Dakota climate. Some

claim that it is nine months winter, three months wind, and the rest summer. Others maintain that it is nine months winter and three months late in the fall. Both sides agree on the length of the winter, and both probably would on the quality of the cold. No less an authority than Stefansson has made the statement that it gets colder in the State of Montana than it does within the Arctic Circle. Our region lies just east of the Montana border, and there is evidence to show that temperature is no respecter of state lines.

Some years ago a member of the fraternity of "sob-brothers," writing about a certain class of workers, asked our tears for them because they worked in a room so chilly that they had to exercise to keep warm. What would he have said had he known that hundreds of herders regularly get wringing wet with sweat legging out bucks and then immediately go out and herd all day in sub-zero weather? If the sob-brother had known that, he would have had the floors of Congress awash with tears, and the senators would have had to go out to the cloakrooms in boats.

And yet herding, like most outdoor jobs, is a healthful one. There is a striking difference in the way cold affects various states and conditions of men. The farm hand comes to breakfast some cold winter morning with his head stuffed up like a sausage and talking through his adenoids. The farmer's wife remarks sympathetically, "You gotta bad cold, have n't you? You 'd oughtta take something for it" — and that is the extent of his medical attention. That night he takes his girl to a distant dance, sweats off three pounds trying to teach his No. 9's to Charleston, goes out between dances to cool off, drives his girl and then himself home during the coldest part of the night, and in a few days is as well as ever. Not so the statesman. He starts out on tour to repair his fences after a political cyclone, and, becoming overheated by his own perfervid oratory, he contracts a slight cold. The newspapers chronicle the fact and add that he is "confined to his room on the orders of his physician." The next day he is slightly worse, and he goes to bed with five doctors and three nurses; complications set in, pneumonia develops, and four days later editors all over the country are pawing through their morgues and deciding which facts to print and which to suppress.

There is a difference of opinion among herders as to whether winter or summer herding is preferable. The majority of them seem to favor winter on account of its shorter days; but personally I take the other side. Many a December 21 has seemed longer to me than the longest day summer ever saw. As I pointed out before, it is possible for a herder to keep reasonably cool through even the hottest summer, but there is many a winter day when it is impossible for him to keep warm.

The great problem for the herder is to wear clothes enough to keep him fairly warm during long periods of inactivity and at the same time to dress lightly enough not to perspire too much when he walks. But, like the man who aimed so as to hit it if it was a deer and miss it if it was a cow, this can't be done. The herder must choose one or the other and his choice will depend on his temperament. Although I choose the heavy dressing for myself, I must admit that one of the most disagreeable of sensations is to have your face fairly stinging with cold and your body bathed in perspiration. It seems as if Nature were attacking you two ways at once.

The sheep do not travel nearly so far in winter as in summer. The deeper the snow, the less inclined they are to ramble. But if a thaw happens to clear the snow off, they make up for lost time and run as they always do in spring. It seems as if they were rejoicing at getting the free use of their legs again. Thaws, and even total disappearance of snow, are not uncommon in winter. In fact, South Dakota weather is as much of a gamble as the radio is. You set the dial and you hear some world-famous pianist in New York thundering out a masterpiece, and then another touch of the knob and your ears are soothed with the refined strains of the "Jackass Blues."

Sheep, like horses, paw snow to graze beneath it. Cattle do not; they eat only what sticks above the snow or what they can nuzzle down to when the snow is soft. Sheep go to work systematically and methodically. They paw four or five times with one front foot, getting down to the grass, and then paw somewhat crosswise to this with the other front foot. Where the two lines cross there is quite a bit of grass exposed, and after cleaning this up they move a step or two and paw again. They are seemingly tireless and bottomless. When the snow is slightly crusted, sheep are still able to paw through it, but when the crust is hard, or when, as often happens, there are two or three crusts, the band must be fed. They do not need water as long as they can get snow. It is all the better if they have access to open water, but when snow is on the ground they can get along without it. This enables the sheepman to get the grass on the high and dry ridges during the winter. On the other hand, in summer the sheep must be where they can water every day; while in spring and fall if they have water every other day they can get along.

There is one product of this region that has gained nation-wide if not world-wide fame, and that is the Dakota blizzard. Whatever the weather does in this part of the country, it does with intense and single-minded earnestness. The force, not to say violence, of the wind may be judged by the fact that when it is due east or west the transcontinental trains frequently blow through our railroad towns as much as a day and a half ahead of schedule. When the country decides to go dry and stay dry — that is, in a strictly aqueous sense — the fishes have their choice of migrating downstream in their native element, or of sticking by the country and playing around in the dust for awhile. When it decides to rain, the culverts come up out of the road for a look around and the bridges play tag with one another down the streams. When the weather decides to be hot, the natives fry their eggs on their doorsteps; and when it decides to be as ornery as it can be, it produces its masterpiece, the blizzard.

Seven years ago there occurred a blizzard which is still referred to as "the March storm."

While this was a storm of unusual violence, it was the same sort of storm that occurs every winter, and usually several times a winter. This particular storm began on a Sunday evening with a light snow and some wind. By daylight the blizzard was in full blast. It raged all that day with unabated fury, and all that night and until about ten o'clock Tuesday morning, thirty-six hours in all. During that time the wagon, although in a comparatively sheltered spot, rocked back and forth like a boat on a rough sea. The air was so full of wet snow that it was almost impossible to face the wind and draw a breath. The weather was not cold, and this is characteristic of blizzards, but the violence of the wind was such that the sting of the wet snow and sleet on the face and hands was unbearable. No beast would face it, and no human being did who could possibly avoid it.

The sheep were in a winter bed ground — that is, where the lie of the land afforded some shelter; but from such a storm as this there was really no protection. Although we went around the sheep, huddled under the bank, every fifteen or twenty minutes during the day, and even up to midnight, yet sometime during the storm the wind whipped two or three hundred head out of the top of the draw and drove them before it into other shelters. We found them after the storm, a few here and a few there, gathered under banks and in low places. The rest were huddled behind the wagon, beside a large drift that had formed during the storm, some of them half buried in it. When we began to pull these out, we noticed steam rising from little holes in the snow near them, and as we dug we found a ewe at the bottom of each of these holes, the steam having been made by her warm breath striking the upper air. Then we set out to dig the snow bank systematically. All that day and parts of the next two we dug sheep out of that bank, some alive and some dead. The third day we dug out a ewe that was so much alive that it took a saddle horse to run her down, when she found she was at liberty once more. Each ewe as we found her was lying in a hollow place about twice her size, where the warmth of her body had melted the surrounding snow. There were many sheep that we missed on account of their being in unexplored parts of the drift ; but altogether that snow bank yielded up thirty-four dead sheep and probably as many live ones. They had huddled close under the bank to be out of the wind ; the outside ones had refused to move, and the inner ones had been gradually drifted under.

But our loss, although heavy, was surpassed by that of others. One sheepman lost nine hundred head out of twelve hundred. The wind had driven them into a swampy place, where they bogged down and chilled to death. Another man, a small farmer, owned twenty-seven head of cattle and a water hole; but when the storm was over he had neither water hole nor cattle. The water hole had happened to be in the south-east corner of his pasture, and the storm had piled the cattle into it and drowned them. In some places the barbs of the wire fences were matted with the bloody hair and flesh of horses, where a bunch of them had been ground along the wires by the force of the wind, the outside horses pressing those inside against the barbs as they milled along the fence.

In counting up the loss from such a storm as this, you must include not only those that die during the storm, but the many others who are so weakened by it that they succumb later. Storms like this, however, are simply one of the factors that must be reckoned with by the inhabitants of this region. All sections of the country have their drawbacks, with the exception of California. Poets have written voluminously about the beauties of winter, but occasionally the thought will obtrude that the bathing beauties of Southern California have a slight edge on the somewhat more frigid beauties of ice and snow. Still, we cannot all lie on the sand and lie about the climate, and dwellers in our region simply accept snow, cold, and blizzards as inescapable accompaniments of winter in the Great Northwest, where for weeks on end the hired man has to thaw out the cow's bag with a blowtorch and milk with his mittens on.

VII

THE BOSS

THERE is one chapter of this book — the one with the above title — that can never be fully written. And that is a pity, for this is one subject on which I feel competent to write a volume complete, with footnotes, appendix, and a glossary of unusual terms. But to steer a safe course between the Scylla of sycophancy and the Charybdis of unemployment requires a bolder and more experienced mariner than the present one. However, although it is not in place to comment on one's own employer, there is no closed season on other bosses.

There was the sheepman, for instance, out in Montana who was putting his sheep on land to which his title was so clouded that it could not be seen at all. He expected trouble and warned his herder, old Andy Swanson.

"Now I 'm going to give you a 30–30 and a lot of ammunition, and if anybody comes bothering you just let him have it."

"Well," replied old Andy, who did not relish being made a cat's paw, "I 'm getting forty-five dollars a month, and I guess that 's not fighting wages."

The question of food furnished to the wagon has probably caused more friction between sheepman and herder than any other one thing. The herder is absolutely at the mercy of his boss in this respect as long as he works for him. Obviously he can't eat what he does n't have. A farm hand eats with the family, faring just as well as they do, and he could hardly ask anything better; but all that the herder eats must be packed and brought out to him.

There was the sheepman, for example, who furnished his herder a can of coffee, a sack of flour, and a slab of fat pork, and told him to cook anything he wanted. On the other hand there was the new herder who was told to look the wagon over and make out an order for the things he needed. The list he sent in looked like a mail-order grocery catalogue copied out with very few omissions. The boss, looking it over carefully, added one item not down, namely, "a new herder."

Then there was the sheepman who was tactfully approached by his herder on the subject of a little meat for the wagon. The sheepman, although a meat eater, was a vegetarian when it came to furnishing the wagon.

"You 've got a gun, have n't you ?" he asked the herder.

"Yes."

"And ammunition ?"

"Yes."

"And there are plenty of rabbits on the prairie, are n't there ?"

"Yes."

"Well, there 's your meat."

A few days later the sheepman on one of his visits to the wagon found a fine ewe dead on her back. He questioned the herder.

"Did you know that ewe was dead there ?"

"No."

"Where were you ?"

"I was out hunting jack rabbits."

However, to the credit of the sheepmen it must be said that the great majority of them keep the wagon well supplied.   There is no real economy, of course, in doing otherwise, because a dissatisfied herder will, by lack of interest in his work, lose much more than the value of the food denied him.   And if he once gets the notion that he has to earn his board and fight for it too, he is likely to begin rehearsing his farewell address, which, if not quite as long as Washington's, is likely to be much more pointed and pithy.

The herder's job is a peculiar one in that he is his own boss a great part of the time.   His work is largely cut out for him, and swift penalties follow any neglect of it.   If through laziness he lets the sheep scatter out too far, he has just so much harder a time getting them together again. The boss comes out once every five or six days in summer, and somewhat oftener than that in winter; but in between times the herder is left to his own devices.   In many ways it is pleasanter than being continually under the eye and direction of somebody else and having your every movement prescribed for you.   No efficiency expert has yet decided which foot the herder should start out with in the morning, nor how much cussing he should be allowed to do under a given set of circumstances.   Such regulation is bound to come in time, as we improve our methods, but meantime the herder has to worry along on his own initiative. When the efficiency expert arrives, the herder can discard his initiative altogether. The expert will have enough for both.

In earlier times herders were often left alone for long periods; in fact, one herder said that if his boss visited him oftener than once in three weeks, he would begin to think his work was n't satisfactory. But it is doubtful whether such conditions exist to-day. Of course the fact that the herder may not see his boss within a given time does not mean that he sees no one. There are always people going and coming on their various errands, and if the herder happens to be near a road he sees cars and passers-by every day. But even so, his job is rightly classed among the solitary ones.

There is one peculiar result of the herder's isolation. Suppose the boss comes out to the wagon and says something the herder does n't like. The boss goes home and promptly forgets it in the numerous contacts he has with others, but the herder does not forget. He mulls it over in his mind, because he has no other immediate contacts to obliterate the memory of this unpleasant one. So he broods over it, and often it curdles the milk of his otherwise sunny disposition. But this is not the fault of the herder; it is merely the result of the conditions of his job.

There is an ever-recurrent story that the laws in certain states compel a sheepman to keep two herders with the bunch all the time, one to herd the sheep and the other to keep the herder from going crazy. What would happen if the ovine influence should upset the mental equilibrium of both of them at the same time is a matter for conjecture. Speaking merely for myself, the sight of someone watching me from day to day for signs of incipient madness would be the surest and quickest way to call to life the germs of that disease which is supposed to lie latent in the herder's calling. And if, in addition, I had to do all the work, while the other fellow confined his labors to his optic nerve, there would inevitably steal into my consciousness the thought that insanity is a valid as well as popular excuse for several of the major crimes.

There is also the fable of another law compelling a sheepman to visit his wagon every so often. This is probably as apocryphal as the other. If this law were amended so as to compel the sheepman to visit his wagon on certain days and on no others, it would receive the strong and hearty support of most herders. As it is, the boss is likely to drop in unannounced almost any time, and this is frequently a cause of embarrassment and deep mortification to the herder, all of

which could be avoided by the simple passage of
this law. There is no doubt that these two laws
will be passed just as soon as the reformers can
get around to it. Just at present they are busy
putting the finishing touches on the prohibition
law, the few little adjustments necessary to
render this noble piece of legislation the air-tight
wonder it was intended to be. In the meantime
the two-herder law and the wagon-visiting law
have the distinction of belonging to that small
and exclusive class of laws that have never been
enacted.

The fact that labor trouble is practically unknown in the relations between sheepman and
herder may be due to various reasons. For one
thing, herders are unorganized. The fact that
one herder would have to walk several miles at
night in order to organize with the next one may
have something to do with that. Then, too,
herders have no itch to parade; in fact, their
ambition is to sit as much and parade as little
as possible. If the sheep cause them to parade
too much, they get distinctly peeved and make
remarks about it. Also, being hired for twenty-
four hours a day, there is no time for them to attend meetings when their twenty-four-hour shift
is over. Besides this, the extent of ground necessary for running a band of sheep is so large, and

the wagons consequently so far apart, that it would take a day and a half to get together enough herders for a good poker game, let alone enough to serve as an audience for inflammatory speeches.

I have still another theory about the herders' lack of an organization, and that is that the nature of the work tends to make them independent. The herder prefers to do his own thinking rather than to pay someone else to do it for him, and he would be very much opposed to supporting some other herder in idleness for this purpose. The first cold day of winter, when he had to keep stamping his feet to maintain an intelligent liaison with them, he would be sure to write to the secretary to discontinue brain-waving for his benefit, and to refund his share of the expenses.

But I think that the real reason for the absence of labor troubles is that sheep raising is still carried on along the old patriarchal lines, and the old man-to-man relation still exists, as it formerly did in almost every occupation. Once in a while a sheepman may suddenly send his herder to join the ranks of the unemployed, or an occasional herder may tell his boss where to shove his sheep, but these are individual cases to be settled each on its own merits. And to counterbalance these melancholy incidents, there are many cases where herders have worked for the same man as long as Jacob did for Laban, even without Jacob's incentive. When a herder has put in ten years working for one man, as I have, it looks as if the boss must be a pretty good guy after all. Modesty forbids the reversal of the formula.

VIII

LAMBING AND SHEARING

THOSE of you who know the devastation that may be wrought in a hitherto peaceful and well-ordered household by the arrival of one little nine-pound stranger are asked to stretch your imaginations and envision the arrival of a thousand or fifteen hundred little strangers at one address within a period of twenty days. It sounds improbable, and yet this is what happens every spring on hundreds of sheep ranches throughout the West. It takes place about the time the green grass has become abundant enough to supply the ewes with milk. As might be expected, all other activity on the ranch ceases while lambing is going on. Extra help is hired, extra hours are added to the working day.

The days themselves are almost at their longest and the boss's temper at its shortest. It is at once the hardest and the most interesting part of the sheepman's year.

There are almost as many ways of conducting a lambing as there are sheepmen. But since each sheepman is convinced that his way is the best, everyone is satisfied. Every method, however, is based on one bed-rock, all-important fact: namely, that for several days after its birth a ewe knows her lamb only by smell. She gradually comes to know its voice, but that takes time. Until she does know it, her lamb must not be kept with too many others, because to find her lamb the ewe has to smell every lamb till she comes to her own, and if she has to smell too many she becomes confused, and may not know her own lamb when she comes to it. Worse still, she may become discouraged and stop looking for it, which, naturally, is fatal to the lamb. For the first day or so, therefore, the ewe and her lamb must be members of a comparatively small bunch.

It is in providing for and manipulating these small bunches that the methods of sheepmen differ. Take, however, the simplest of all plans as an illustration. The "drop bunch," composed of the ewes that are to lamb, is driven

slowly, day by day, along the banks of a stream.
The wagon follows, being set in a different spot
each night.   Every morning the lambs born during the night are separated from the rest of the
bunch with their mothers and are left behind.
Every evening, likewise, the lambs born during
the day are cut out and left where the drop
bunch was held that day, so the bunch goes
"clean" to the new bed ground.   Each day's
"drop" and each night's drop are left undisturbed for about twenty-four hours.   Then a
day's drop will be combined with a night's drop
and left for another twenty-four hours, when it
will be combined with another bunch of the same
size and as nearly as possible the same age.   A
day or two later this combined group will be put
with another similarly constituted, and so the
building-up process goes on.   Meanwhile the ewe
is learning to find her lamb in an ever larger bunch
and is getting his voice firmly fixed in her mind.
Once she is certain of that, she will find her lamb
among two thousand.   The building-up process
goes on till there are four or five hundred lambs,
and then this bunch is given a special herder and
another lamb bunch is started.   However, when
this second bunch has reached a hundred or two,
it is added to the big lamb bunch, and this pro-
cedure is followed till all but the few inevitable

"drys" have lambed.   These too are finally put
with the rest, and lambing is over.

It must be noted that sheep nature differs
vastly from that of a horse or cow.   A cow knows
where her calf is every minute.   If he is not at
her side, she probably has him cached somewhere.
But she knows just where he is.   Similarly a
young colt rarely leaves his mother's side.   But a
lamb is different.   As soon as he has sucked, he
lies down and promptly goes to sleep.   His
mother wanders about as she grazes.   When she
wishes to find him, she smells of the lamb nearest
to her.   If he is not the one, she smells of the
next, and so on until she reaches her own.   Of
course she calls for him continually.

Having taken a look at the general outline of
lambing, let us view it at closer quarters, first
from the standpoint of the individual ewe.   An
hour or so before the lamb is born the ewe stops
grazing and begins to think exclusively about
her lamb.   She walks about calling for it, and
takes a great interest in other lambs, especially
those that are newborn.   The curious part of
it is that she does n't know whether her lamb
has been born or not.   She tries to mother the
lambs of other ewes, and when some jealous ewe
shoulders her away, she goes to some other ewe's
lamb.   But usually as soon as her own lamb is

born uncertainty vanishes, and she devotes herself exclusively to him.

When a lamb is born, he is frequently a bright orange color. In fact, he is the most conspicuous object in the landscape. Is n't this, perhaps, Nature's way of insuring that the ewe will find him? It seems reasonable to suppose so, because this bright color fades to a rusty brown in the course of an hour or two, and by that time the lamb is either mothered up or doomed.

As the ewe stands above her newborn lamb, she utters a sound that she has not used for a year, a low rumble in the throat, made without opening the mouth. This rumble is used only by a ewe talking to her lamb, or by a buck talking to a ewe, and therefore must denote deep affection. The lamb bleats, the ewe rumbles. Of course if the lamb is at a distance, or is temporarily mislaid, as he is half the time, the ewe calls for him with a full open-mouthed bleat. Once in a while you will see a ewe in search of her lamb going through all the motions of bleating without uttering a sound. She has been calling her lamb so long that she has entirely lost the use of her voice. Yet she is still making the attempt to call. After she finds her lamb and rests her vocal chords, her voice comes back.

During the first hour of the lamb's life the ewe

pays him closer attention than she ever will again.
She licks him, she answers his every bleat with a
rumble, she anxiously superintends his first attempts to stand and his first meal. This hour is
the most critical period of the lamb's whole life.
If he gets to his feet and sucks, he has a good
chance; if he does not, he is doomed, barring
human aid. Following this time of intense anxi-
ety on the ewe's part, her interest in the lamb
steadily declines, until at weaning time it
reaches zero. Paralleling this, the lamb's de-
pendence on her decreases in exactly the same
ratio. In his first hour of life he is absolutely
dependent on her. For many days it is she
who must keep track of him; he does not
know her from any other ewe. Later he comes
to assume half the responsibility for their finding
one another. At weaning time the lamb no
longer needs his mother; she no longer cares for
him.

A newborn lamb is one of the least beautiful
objects on earth. Only the mother of a homely
child can ever know what a ewe sees attractive in
her awkward, ungainly offspring, all legs, ears,
and appetite. He wabbles around unsteadily,
shows a perfect willingness to follow any ewe that
passes, and is perpetually getting lost and raising
a disturbance about it. When he is ten feet

away from his mother and headed in the wrong direction, he is lost. So he stands there and squalls, and keeps right on squalling until his mother comes to him. A little later he will show more initiative and look for her as well as call, but for the present his whole idea is to stand still and make a noise. And if anyone thinks that even a day-old lamb can't make a noise, he is cordially invited to come out and investigate. But he had better bring his ear muffs along.

Although a newborn lamb is skinny, awkward, homely, and ungainly, by the time he is a week or two old he is as pretty as a picture. He is filled out, knows how to handle himself, and can run like a deer and jump like a goat. He is full of fun and likes to play games with the other lambs, "king on the mountain" being one of the favorites. He will stand on a hummock and defy all comers, knocking his playmates off it until he himself is pushed off by some sturdier lamb. He will run along the face of a cut bank with a hundred or more of his fellows, wheel around, and run back again. But his real dissipation comes when he finds an old road, preferably one with a number of ruts. He and several hundred of his friends will tear along this road in a close bunch as if their very lives depended on it, and then, when they have run so far that you begin to think that they are leaving altogether, they will turn around and tear back again, and keep this up until their little tongues are hanging out and they themselves are all in. Then they will break up and run back to the bunch, each one hunting up his mother. Once in a while you will see some overanxious ewe running alongside them in their flight trying to keep track of Little Woolly, but for the most part the ewes seem to reflect that "lambs will be lambs" and to feel confident that their youngsters will return to them when they grow tired or hungry.

And this confidence is well founded. For, whatever the lamb means to the ewe, it is abundantly evident that the ewe means to the lamb just one thing, and that is milk, frequently, in a hurry, and lots of it. The lamb sucks every time he thinks about it, and he thinks about it so constantly that he may almost be said to have a single-track mind. The whole process of getting his dinner is so stereotyped that you might watch him a hundred times or watch a hundred different lambs and there would be no variation in the ceremony. The lamb arrives on the run (he is always in a hurry at mealtime), throws himself on his knees at his mother's side, but facing in the opposite direction, and starts in. The ewe invariably smells of the part of him nearest to her in order to be sure that he is the right lamb, and then looks in the direction of the dog, or the herder, or any possible source of danger. When she thinks that dinner is or ought to be over, she merely takes a step or two forward, and this leaves the lamb on his knees staring into space. He philosophically accepts the inevitable, gets up, and invariably shakes his head. This has the effect of shaking off the drop or two of milk that may cling to his lips, which if left there would sour and become the breeding place of flies. Thus does Nature care for her own.

Here it becomes a painful duty to record some of the darker sides of lamb nature. You see a lamb walking through the bunch calling for his mother. Nothing unusual in that. But a little way behind him another lamb is following, step for step. Mark him well, for he is the villain of the piece. This second lamb is n't calling at all. He looks quite guileless and innocent, but his head is slightly darker than the rest of him, and his heart, if we could see it, is darker still with thoughts of theft and highway robbery. By this time the first lamb has located his mother and is advancing on the run. The other lamb keeps right behind him. At the precise moment when the first lamb throws himself on his knees and begins to suck, the second one seizes from behind the teat on the other side and begins extracting milk with a rapidity which only a lamb can equal.   In the second or two while the bewildered ewe is trying to decide whether or not she really did have twins, the "moocher," for that is his name, has extracted several swallows of milk.   The next instant the ewe kicks free of both lambs and walks away a little distance.   The two lambs follow in the same order as before, but this time the ewe is on her guard.   The instant the moocher touches the teat, the mother is gone again.   It is no use to follow any farther, as the dejected moocher well knows, and he strolls away in search of a new victim.   Because he always approaches from the rear, the wool on his head becomes discolored, and, like Cain, he bears the brand of his infamy on his brow.   All men know him for a moocher, which is considerably more than can be said for his human counterpart.   Occasionally a lamb is driven to this evil course because his own mother does not have enough milk and consequently he is always hungry, but in other cases his actions can only be accounted for on the theory of original sin.   Sometimes, to judge from appearances, he does quite well by himself.

Another fault that must be laid at the door of most lambs is a lack of consideration for the feel-

ings of their mothers.   The lamb early finds out
that butting the udder with his head is a very
good way of encouraging a generous flow of milk.
But he carries this idea to extremes, for a half-
grown lamb will frequently butt with such force
that he lifts both hind legs of the ewe clear of
the ground.   Now presumably the average ewe
never studied physics, and does not know that
when an object in motion changes direction it
loses force; yet many a ewe will turn at right
angles just as the lamb arrives, and the latter,
instead of hurling himself at the udder head-on,
like a woolly battering-ram, finds himself obliged
to creep around on his knees to a new position
and a more civil behavior.

Up to this point we have been considering
lambing as it is when everything goes well.   That
it does not always do so is a cause of much sorrow
and profanity to the boss and the lambing crew.
In fact there are so many things that can and do
go wrong that the nerves and tempers of all are
tried to the utmost.   The commonest trouble is
that a ewe refuses to own her lamb.   This may
result from a variety of causes.   If, for example,
a ewe mothers another lamb before the birth of
her own, she may become so attached to the first
lamb that she will neglect hers entirely.   Cases
of this kind are by no means uncommon.

Fortunately the remedy is simple.   The ewe and her own lamb are transferred to another bunch, and there she soon forgets about the other lamb and devotes herself to her own.

Then there is the ewe who, while owning her lamb, does not feel like giving up her social duties in order to take care of him — that is, she persists in following the bunch, and as the lamb cannot keep up the pace at that early age, he is left behind.   The remedy for this is to hobble the social gadder, thus making it impossible for her to move at other than a snail's pace, while leaving her free to graze.   The lamb easily keeps up with her slow progress, and as soon as the ewe shows evidence of being willing to carry out her family duties she is set at liberty again.

Then there is the old ewe that has no milk.   It is a remarkable provision of Nature that a ewe in this condition rarely shows any affection for her lamb.   She cannot raise him and she has no interest in him.   In this case there is nothing to do but let the ewe go and either kill the lamb or raise it by hand.

But sometimes it is possible to give one ewe's lamb to another ewe.   Suppose a ewe who is a good mother and has plenty of milk gives birth to a dead lamb, and the same day a lamb is born to a ewe that has no milk.   The practice is to skin the dead lamb and pull this skin over the live lamb, as you would pull on a sweater. This double-skinned lamb is then shut up with the dead lamb's mother. The ewe smells the topmost skin, and very often accepts the lamb as her own. The skin is left on, and by the time it is dried up and useless the ewe has become accustomed to the smell of the foster lamb and raises him as hers. This does not always work, but where it does it means one lamb saved. Sometimes in the case of a ewe very anxious for a lamb, it is enough to squirt some of her milk on the head of the lamb to be adopted.

I saw one case of deliberate lamb stealing. A ewe had lost her lamb shortly after it was born ; it was from the first not destined to live — a spindling, puny thing. Nevertheless she walked all over calling for it. The next time I saw her, she was mothering another lamb, whose own mother was also along. When I next saw her, and ever after that, she had the lamb to herself. The best mother had won.

A lamb that cannot be raised by his mother, whatever the reason, is called a "bum." These bums are either killed, given away, or raised by hand at the ranch. Many a man has gotten a start in sheep by securing bum lambs from neighboring sheepmen. It is quite a little trouble to raise them, as they have to be fed five times a day at the start, three times a day later on, and this is kept up all summer.   But on the other hand, the only expense is a little milk, and the reward is a six- or seven-dollar lamb in the fall.   Sometimes lambs are raised on bottles with the regulation nipples, but the more general practice is to teach them to drink out of a pan, which in itself is no easy job.

It is a strange fact that lambs brought up around the house and in more or less close touch with human beings become quite different from the ordinary range sheep in their habits and disposition.   They develop strong individuality, one might almost say personality.   It would be an interesting question to determine whether this individuality is latent in all sheep and brought out by their new environment, or whether it really exists in the ordinary range sheep and is noted only when the chance for closer observation has come.

Sometimes these bum lambs have been known to do remarkable things.   A sheepman had been conducting an agricultural experiment involving the soaking of rye and yeast and sugar in a barrel. Having brought the experiment to a highly successful conclusion, he dumped the mash — I mean the residue — out behind the barn.   He had at the ranch a puny little bum lamb that he did n't know whether he would be able to raise or not. One evening he noticed, while he was doing chores, that the lamb was hanging around the pile of residue, sampling it from time to time. He noted that it had a kind of cockeyed look, and staggered slightly when it walked. The next morning at daybreak he was wakened by a terrible commotion in the barnyard, and he jumped out of bed and ran to the window just in time to see the lamb overtake, pull down, and tear to pieces a big wolf that had been hanging around the ranch and doing considerable damage; and later on in the day he found the mangled carcasses of two other wolves. It sounds improbable, but it must be so, for an account of it appeared in the local paper.

We once had a lamb born on a snow bank during the latter part of winter. He came in with the bunch that night under his own steam, following a ewe who turned out to have been his mother by adoption only. His own mother could not be found. Because he had ventured somewhat hardily into a cold world, he was named after that other famous arctic explorer, Dr. Cook, and was called Freddy for short. Since it was still winter, he was given the run of the house, and he quickly discovered that the warmest nook in it was between the kitchen range and the wall, and there he spent much of his time. With the coming of spring, much to his disgust, Freddy was banished from the house, but he would hang around the kitchen door and sneak in at every opportunity, only to be promptly thrown out again as soon as discovered. One sweltering day in summer, a wash day, the screen door happened to be open, and Freddy slipped in unobserved and went to his favorite spot behind the stove. Some time later he made the only voluntary exit of his career, and he made it none too soon. As he emerged from behind the stove he was panting, his little tongue was hanging out, the wool on top of his head was scorched brown, and from it a tiny wisp of smoke was beginning to rise. This little taste of the hereafter seemed to have its effect. At any rate he never again tried to enter the house.

If a ewe has great difficulty in giving birth to a lamb, the chances are that she will desert him. In this case she is caught and shut up with him, and usually she will recognize and take care of him. It is a peculiar fact that on raw, cold days, particularly if the grass is poor and the sheep consequently hungry, there will be several ewes that desert their lambs. This brings about an almost total loss of religion on the part of the lambers, for every such ewe must be run down and caught and either taken to a pen or a pen brought to her.   Meanwhile of course the sheep are traveling and other lambs are being born. The best days for lambing are the still, hot ones. Then desertions are comparatively rare.

Occasionally a young healthy ewe with plenty of milk will refuse to own her lamb, for some reason known only to herself.   Then the real struggle begins.   She and the lamb are shut up in a small pen together and left there.   She is given feed and water, and three or four times a day the lamb is forcibly fed — that is, the ewe is forced to let him suck.   She may be kept this way for several days with nothing in the world to think about but that lamb.   Frequently she finally gives in, and allows the lamb to get his food in the way Nature intended.

Sometimes in a final effort to make a ewe own her lamb, a dog is brought close to the pen.   If the ewe has any spark of maternal feeling in her, this will bring it out.   When she at last accepts the lamb, she rumbles in her throat and permits him to suck.   It is then safe to turn her out with him.

But sometimes nothing will induce her to own him.   There was the case of Princess.   She had been raised as a pet, probably having been deserted by her own mother, and therefore having the taint of lamb desertion in her blood. She raised her first lamb nicely and took good care of him. But having done this much, she seemed to feel that she had done her whole duty by the race — a questionable position, but one with much human precedent to back it. At any rate, when her next lamb was born, Princess absolutely refused to have anything to do with him. In the face of all the evidence she insisted that she had n't had a lamb, that she did n't want a lamb, and that she certainly did n't intend to raise a lamb. The boss, in language unfit for the ears of any real lady, let alone a princess, informed her that she would either raise that lamb or spend the rest of her life in captivity with it. The feminine readers of this don't need to be told how it all turned out. For the benefit of the others I will explain that the lamb was raised by hand.

There is still another kind of ewe that makes trouble for the lambers, and that is a two-year-old. On the Western ranges a ewe has her first lamb at two. Often she does not know how to take care of it; sometimes she deserts it. I happened to see a two-year-old, a pet named Nellie, shortly after her first lamb was born. She and the lamb stood facing one another.

Nellie was plainly at a loss. Here was the lamb, a *fait accompli*, but just what to do about it she did n't know. So she followed the experimental method and tried two kinds of treatment: first she licked the lamb and then she knocked it down; then when the lamb got up and came toward her she licked it awhile and then knocked it down again. After the third or fourth knock-down the lamb got "goosy," and would jump sidewise when Nellie approached him. I left her wrestling with the problem. The next time I saw her she had come to the conclusion that she was the sole proprietor of the finest lamb that was ever born, and everybody was happy, especially the lamb.

While in the East twin lambs are rather the rule than otherwise, in the West they are distinctly the exception, and different sheepmen have various ways of dealing with them. Some make a practice of killing or giving away the weaker of the two lambs, on the theory that it is better to have one good lamb than two poor ones. Others put all ewes with twins in a small pasture, and a very high percentage of lambs can be saved by this method. Others let the twins take their chances in the main bunch, but the odds are all against them there, and only the exceptional ewe will bring them both through to shipping time.

It is again a remarkable provision of Nature that a ewe with twins will not let either of them suck by himself.   Both must be there and suck at the same time.   Otherwise of course the greedier of the two would quickly starve the other to death.

The instinct of a young lamb is a wonderful thing.   A half hour after he is born he knows enough to curl up in the lee of a sage bush rather than on its exposed side.   It takes very few lessons to teach him that it is safer and pleasanter to walk around a cactus bed rather than over it. His first act in life is to get something to eat, and he knows just where to look for it.   But here he soon gets into difficulties, because of the fact that one lunch counter looks as good to him as another.   He plays no favorites.   Like an anti-Prohibitionist he does n't care where he gets his drink, as long as he gets it.   The ewes, however, are not so broad-minded, and it costs the young lamb many a knockdown before he learns that the boarding house run by his mother, with its warm meals at all hours, is the only one where he is welcome.

When the lambs are very young, the ewes seem to spend about half their time chasing other ewes' lambs away.   Some of them are so jealous of their own lamb's privileges that they will not only knock down any other lamb that ventures within reach, but will then drop on their knees, put their heads against the interloper, and apparently try to grind him into the earth. But this violent phase never lasts very long. I have never seen a ewe resent the treatment accorded her lamb by another ewe. She will hover around, anxiously calling him, but will make no move to protect or avenge him.

Yearlings like to play with young lambs, but their ideas of sport cannot make much of an appeal to the lambs. It is somewhat like a tough kid of twelve trying to play with his four-year-old brother on equal terms. In fact, yearlings are so rough with lambs that most sheepmen take them out of the bunch altogether during lambing, running them in separate bands by themselves. The ewes could easily protect their lambs from the yearlings, but it does not seem to occur to them to do so.

Toward a dog, however, the ewe, timid as she is during most of the year, at lambing time assumes an attitude of defiance. She will snort, stamp her foot, and, if she thinks the dog will run, will even chase him, though just what she would do with him if she caught him is a matter for conjecture.

To attend to all the details of lambing requires quite a crew of men. They are called "lambers," or, derisively, "lamb lickers," because they are said to aid the ewe in her maternal duties and to have their tongues split in order to do this more efficiently.   But this is a base canard, like saying that the people of Oregon have webbed feet on account of the excessive rainfall.   The lambers are supplied with sheep hooks to enable them to catch the ewes when necessary.   These are not the shepherds' crooks, familiar in Bible illustrations, but are straight ash sticks, the thickness of a broom handle and about eight feet long, with steel hooks on the end.   These hooks are so shaped that they will just slip past the thinnest part of the ewe's leg, but will not pull off over the hoof.   The trick is to keep a strain on the pole after the sheep is hooked, so as to prevent her from kicking out.   The idea is the same as keeping a taut line after hooking a fish.

There are several divisions to lambing work. One man, usually the regular herder, holds the drop bunch.   His duty is to see that every lamb that is born is mothered up, and if it is n't, to catch the mother and put her with it in a lambing teepee.   This is a miniature tent, just big enough to hold a ewe and her lamb comfortably. In bad weather it is sometimes necessary to teepee every lamb as it is born.   In this case there will usually be two men with the drop bunch, one to hold the bunch, and the other to do the teepeeing.

Then there are one or more wranglers, according to the number of sheep in the band. The wranglers have various duties, one of which is to visit the different small bunches and see that they contain the right number of ewes and lambs. While the bunches are small the wrangler knows the number of lambs there ought to be in each one. If there is a lamb short in any bunch, he is probably lying down in the tall grass somewhere, so the wrangler hunts him up and restores him to his mother. He also sees to it that the individual lambs are all right It often happens that a lamb is unable to start the milk. In such a case he quickly assumes the general proportions of a living skeleton. The wrangler sees what is wrong, catches the ewe, starts the milk in each teat, suckles the lamb, and sets him on the high road to recovery. If the ewe has no milk, or if the wrangler cannot determine which is the mother, the lamb becomes a bum.

Another duty of the wrangler is to "work the bed ground." When the drop bunch leaves in the morning, all the lambs are put back together with all the ewes that have lambed. Most of them will be paired up all right, a ewe and a lamb, but there will be some ewes without lambs and *vice versa*.   It is the wrangler's first business to straighten them out, to decide from their general appearance which ewe belongs to which lamb, and then to put them together in pens to see if his guess was correct.   He also suckles the lambs that look as if they had not yet had any milk.   If the morning is very cold or rainy, there will be one or more lambs chilled down.   For these the wrangler must build a fire in the sheep-wagon stove, lay some sacks on the oven door, and put the lambs as nearly inside the stove as he can without actually cooking them.   It is amazing how much heat a chilled lamb can stand.   After an hour or two of this roasting the lamb gradually comes to life, gets to his feet, calls for his mother, and is ready to be restored to her.

But the hardest part of a wrangler's job is the moving of lamb bunches.   From one to three of them must be moved every day.   They say it takes all kinds of people to make a world, and the wrangler finds almost every kind of ewe and lamb in every lamb bunch.   There is the ewe with a lamb who is a good traveler, and her one idea is to take that lamb and travel as fast and as far as possible.   She must be continually headed back into the bunch.   Then there is the ewe who is afraid that her lamb can't walk at all,

so she walks backward step by step in front of
him and delays the procession.   There is the ewe
with an obsession that she ought to go east,
when the wrangler wants her to go south.
Then there is the lamb that is a little weak and
lies down every time the wrangler turns his back
on him.   There is the lamb that does n't know
how to walk, does n't want to learn, and that
won't walk after he does learn.   Finally, there is
the lamb that persists in mistaking the wrangler
for his mother, and keeps struggling towards him
instead of walking from him.   No wonder that
the wrangler gradually loses his sunny disposition, his patience, his temper, and his religion.
After all, Job was spared a few of the toughest
trials.

But the worst thing that can happen during
lambing is a "mix" — that is, the mixing of two
lamb bunches before the proper time, usually the
result of carelessness.   It is the one thing that
will bring the sheepman out of the ranch house
orrey-eyed, waving a check in one hand and a
shotgun loaded with soup beans in the other
— the check intended to terminate the unlucky lamber's engagement, and the soup beans
to hasten his departure.   For a mix invariably
means bum lambs, and a bum lamb means a
five-dollar loss.

Besides the drop-bunch herder and the wranglers, there is sometimes a night man. He goes through the bunch at frequent intervals during the night and sees that every new lamb is mothered up, or, if not, he finds the mother and pens the two. In case of a storm he pens every ewe with her lamb as soon as it is born. But the night man is used only where the sheep are corralled. It is not practical to use him on an open bed ground.

Finally, about the middle of lambing, a new man is added, to herd the big lamb bunch. There are four or five hundred lambs by now, and they need all of one man's time. His duties are practically those of a herder. While the drop bunch is growing smaller day by day, the lamb bunch is continually getting bigger. When there is only a remnant of the drop bunch left, it too is thrown into the lamb bunch, and lambing is over.

Suppose we take a sample day during lambing. The drop bunch is bedded away from the wagon, and the drop-bunch herder and the wrangler are sleeping beside it in a round-up bed. They get up a little before sunrise, and when the sheep are ready to leave, they cut back the new-born lambs and their mothers. While the herder takes the drop bunch to the place where they are to graze that day, the wrangler goes to the wagon and gets breakfast. He eats his own, then, leaving the herder's on the back of the stove, he goes out to the bunch to let the herder come in. The latter eats his breakfast, washes the dishes, and goes out to the drop bunch again, and the wrangler starts on his daily round. After working the bed ground, as before described, he begins to move lamb bunches, probably moving two during the forenoon. About eleven o'clock he goes to the wagon and gets dinner. Being human, he spends as much time at it as he thinks safe, and does not go out to relieve the herder till nearly one o'clock. The latter gives him a dirty look, but does n't say anything, because his revenge is easy and obvious. It is nearly three o'clock when the herder gets back to the drop bunch. There is only time for the wrangler to move one lamb bunch in what remains of the afternoon. Then he goes to the wagon and cooks supper. But the wrangler and the herder are anxious to wind up the day's work, so there is no dawdling over the evening meal. As soon as it is over, both men cut out the lambs born during the day, and the herder takes the drop bunch to the appointed bed ground, while the wrangler throws the day's drop closer together and sets up scarecrows around them. Some time during the day the boss comes out and gives his orders for the next twenty-four hours, moves the round-up bed, and goes back to the ranch, where one or two of the larger lamb bunches are being taken care of. Another day and another two dollars.

Working hours during lambing are such as would give a labor-union leader heart failure or apoplexy, or both. Work begins at five in the morning, if not earlier, and, if everything goes well, it is over by eight at night. If things go wrong, the work runs as late as is necessary. The answer to this is of course that the whole job is a seasonal one and runs only about twenty days in the year, and a person can stand almost anything for that length of time. But it is interesting to note that while some sheep shearers start down by the Mexican border in the early spring and follow the shearing season up into Canada months later, there is no record of a lamber hankering to go through with more than one lambing in the course of a year. The same men are likely to lamb year after year, but one good dose of it seems to suffice for at least twelve months.

It is the custom when a weak or sick ewe must be left out on the prairie to tie a rag or handkerchief around her neck, so that the herder may know by that mark when he has picked her up. Several years ago we had a half-grown boy named

Johnny on the lambing crew, and one day he said that he had marked an old ewe and left her by a certain cutbank.   Next day he asked me if I had seen her.   I was much surprised at the question, for after a lamber has marked a ewe, has cussed her out for causing him that trouble, and has reported where he left her, he usually considers that he has done his whole duty by her.   The next day Johnny asked me again if I had picked her up.   My admiration was increasing by leaps and bounds.   Here, I thought, is a conscientious fellow who is destined some day to revolutionize lambing customs.   I told him I had not seen her. The day following, when Johnny had asked again and had received the same answer, he thought a moment, and then said, his voice trembling with real emotion, "If I 'd knowed that old ewe was going to go and get lost with my new fifty-cent handkerchief, I 'd 'a' knocked her on the head !"

"A sheep shearer is a sheep herder with his brains knocked out."   Something tells me that this definition, current in the sheep country, originated with a sheep herder rather than a sheep shearer.   Certainly I never heard a shearer quote it or subscribe to it, but, as a herder, I could much more easily believe it than I could the reverse saying, which is also sometimes heard.

But whatever the division of brains between the two, there is no dispute as to the division of wages. The sheep shearer is the wage-earning aristocrat of the Western plains. Since fifteen cents per head is the present price for shearing, and since a good shearer can turn out from a hundred to a hundred and fifty sheep a day, the resultant daily wage of fifteen to twenty dollars might make even a New York bricklayer's mouth water. If he knew that free bed and board went with this also, he would inevitably tear up his union card and follow his late fellow townsman's advice to go West.

The fly in this particular bottle of ointment is that shearing, like lambing, is a strictly seasonal job. Having once taken the wool off a ewe, the shearer is through with that particular sheep for the next twelve months; and this condition is likely to obtain until the shearers, like their first cousins, the barbers, are able to persuade their clients to have their wool trimmed in a different way every two or three weeks. At present the shearing season lasts about a month. There are always some sheepmen who wish to shear early, so as to give the ewes plenty of time to get their winter clothes ready; and others habitually shear late, so as to get as much wool as possible for the current year.

Although his wages are so high, any shearer will tell you that he does n't make any money. But there is a suspicion that the motive back of such a statement is the discouragement of possible competition rather than a desire for strict financial accuracy. Certainly if the shearer at fifteen dollars a day does not make any money, the harvest hand at five dollars must be headed straight for bankruptcy. However this may be, it is certain that every spring all the shearers that are not "hog-tied" by other considerations organize themselves into shearing crews of six to a dozen men, elect a captain, and go out after the business. The crew that lands the greatest number of shearing jobs is considered the most successful, so if it really is true that they don't make any money, the shearers do a great injustice to their backs, without reflecting any great credit on their heads.

For shearing is the hardest kind of hard work. No one who has watched shearers at work will be inclined to doubt that they earn their money. The fact that they make a practice of changing their sweat-soaked clothing before each meal is proof enough of that. And these working clothes are apt to be the scantiest that decency will allow. In the very hottest weather, the shearers have to lay off for an hour or so at a time, because they cannot stand the grueling work in combination with intense heat. Neither can they stand long working hours, about eight of these seeming to suffice them.

There are two kinds of shearers, hand men and machine men. The former, as their name indicates, shear directly by hand, using a distinctive implement called sheep shears, which are much like the shears used to trim hedges. Machine men work with power shears run by a gas engine, operating exactly like the electric clippers in a barber shop. Machine men shear somewhat faster than hand men, and the resultant sheep look smoother. On the other hand, many sheepmen believe that the machines take off too much of the wool, not leaving enough to keep the skin from being blistered, or to serve as a foundation for the winter fleece. It is largely a question of personal preference. Some stick to the machines, some to the hand men, while others waver back and forth between the two. There are arguments and argufiers on both sides, and doubtless will continue to be.

The machine crews who travel around to the various ranches, as most crews do, carry with them little portable engines, each furnishing power for two men. Where there are permanent shearing pens and many bands of sheep are trailed to them to be sheared, there is usually one large engine with a line shaft, from which power pulleys go down to each pen. Machine men never tie their fleeces, as this would leave engine power running to waste, but hand crews invariably tie theirs.

Shearing might almost be classed among the exact sciences. A shearer will use the same method and the same strokes with every sheep. There is nothing aimless or haphazard about his work. Each stroke is the best one to make at that point, and there is no waste motion. The whole process is the result of the best experience of the past.

There is always a tendency for the shearers to get rough with a sheep that shows fight and thereby hampers their efforts, yet they show an unexpected tender-heartedness when one of their crew is a beginner. Some one of the shearers is sure to offer to go out and pluck a little grass to keep the ewe from starving to death before her shearing is completed. The fact that a beginner is lucky to shear fifteen or twenty sheep the first day gives point to this. Another shearer will offer to get a basket so that the new man can collect the wool after he has removed it.

There was a bachelor in our neighborhood who had a very large pet sheep and a very small

pair of scissors with which to shear him.   He
spent the best part of three days in removing
the fleece, with time out for necessary rest and
refreshment.   The remarkable thing is that both
he and the sheep survived.

Naturally there must be an extra crew of
men at this time to handle the sheep, to bring
them to the shearers and take them away again.
There are two wranglers whose business it is to
see that there are always unshorn sheep in the
pens of the shearers.   "Sheep out !" is the cry
that warns them that some shearer has just
grabbed the last unshorn sheep in his pen.
They hustle over to him, count the pen, verify
it with the shearer's count, turn the sheared
sheep out, and bring an equal number of un-
sheared ones in.   This must all be done before
the shearer is ready for his next sheep.   The
sheared sheep go into a somewhat larger pen,
and when there are a sufficient number in it
they receive a fresh brand.

A cow or horse brand is burned into the animal's hide, and once put on is there to stay.   But
a sheep brand is merely paint-stamped on the
wool and therefore must be renewed after every
shearing, and usually once in between times,
when it may have become indistinct.   Since
the use of paint allows of a difference in color

as well as the shape of the brand, there is afforded an added protection where bands belonging to different men are run side by side. If one brand is green, for instance, and the other black, any smallest part of the brand is sufficient to prove the ownership of the sheep.

Since the paint affects only the tip of the wool, it would seem an easy matter for anyone so disposed to clip the brand off and substitute another for it. Several citizens who at one time or another have had that idea are at present the guests of the State in one of its handsomest and strongest buildings, with ample leisure to think things over and find out where the fallacy lay.

Besides the wranglers, there is sometimes a wool tier, and always a wool tramper. Since machine men do not tie their own fleeces, one man is hired to do this for the whole crew. It is the business of the wool tramper to tramp the fleeces as solidly as possible into the six-foot sacks that carry them to market. The sacks are suspended free of the ground in a frame, and the wool tramper, starting at the bottom, rises as his sack fills; and to the natural grease in the wool he contributes freely of his own sweat. But this is of no benefit to him, since the sheepman gets paid for whatever weight the wool tramper loses. The only glory the wool tramper has is that when he is standing on top of a full sack on a hot day at the top of the shed beneath a tin roof, he is occupying the hottest spot in the universe, except one.

The one thing dreaded during shearing by all concerned is rain. Wool cannot be sacked (and consequently cannot be sheared) when it is wet. So when the rain interrupts shearing, as it frequently does, everything stops but the interest on the mortgage and the activities of the women. Strange as it may seem, shearers eat just as heartily when loafing around as they do when earning twenty dollars a day. It is no exaggeration to say that the women hate rain worse than any of the others do, for every day of rain means another day of feeding ten or twelve extra men. I might add that the wages of the women not only do not average twenty dollars a day, but do not even total half that much. Besides which, convention does not allow them to employ their leisure in trying to take money from one another via the poker route, as is the pleasant custom of the shearers and wranglers. The complete emancipation of woman has not yet arrived, at least not this far West.

During shearing the lambs have to be separated from their mothers before the latter are put in the pens. Lambs are much too lively and too apt to interfere with the work of the shearers. But the whole band must be turned together at noon as well as at night, in order that the lambs may not go too long without food. It is amusing to watch a lamb trying to find its mother for the first time after she has been sheared. He will come running at her call and then go right past her, failing utterly to recognize her. He has never seen her in this dishabille. He might well be excused for not knowing her, for in her new Eve-like garments she is as homely an object as is to be seen. She is blotched all over with irregular patches of purple, yellow, and black, and she carries various unornamental cuts and gashes, souvenirs of her recent visit to the shearers. Any anatomical defects that she may have stand out with painful clearness, and the sight of twelve hundred of her kind leaving the shearing pens in their all but utter reveal- ment is calculated to make the thoughtful flapper wend her way homeward and put on some clothes.

IX

SHEEP AND HERDER TRAITS

THERE are two common misconceptions about
sheep on the part of almost everyone who is not
directly concerned with them: one is that they
are long-tailed, and the other that they are white.
Now whatever may have been the condition of
Little Bo-Peep's bunch, there are very few long-
tailed sheep on the range. There are good and
valid reasons, which cannot be stated here, for
removing the tails. In fact the prejudice of
buyers and feeders against long-tails is so strong
that when any of them show up in the stockyards
their owners have to take twenty-five cents a
head less for them than for the others. Consequently the tails are removed when the lambs

are about ten days old — docking, it is called.
At the same time the lambs are earmarked —
that is, one ear or the other is split or cropped,
making four possible earmarks, and these are
used in regular rotation.   In this way the sheepman is enabled to cut out all sheep of a certain
age simply by their earmarks.

All this may seem somewhat cruel, but it is
no more so than the branding and earmarking
of cattle, and in both cases there is the valid
excuse of necessity.   There was a kind-hearted
and well-meaning man in England who introduced a bill into Parliament a short while ago to
compel the owners of live stock to put them
under an anæsthetic when performing these
operations.   This   tender-hearted   enthusiast,
after administering the anæsthetic to the five
hundredth lamb, would be in splendid condition for an operation or two on himself.

The other popular misconception regarding
sheep is that they are white.   The fact is that
they rarely approach that color.   On account of
the dust and grease in their wool they are usually
a rich yellow, like cream.   If they are corralled
every night, they soon become almost black, and
of course there are sheep of all shades in between.
After a heavy rain, which washes all the dirt
out of the wool, they are as nearly white as they

ever become.   We think of them as white, but
they stand out against a snow bank like a
colored gentleman in a Klan convention.

Sheep have their own peculiar likes and dislikes.   They do not like to go straight up a hill
or straight down one.   They are great climbers,
like their cousins, the goats, but they like to
angle up or down.   They have a profound dislike for going over the brow of a hill or through
tall grass or anywhere that they cannot see their
way clear.   They are by nature timid animals,
and they seem to have a dread of what they may
see "on the other side."   When being driven,
they will go up close to the top of a hill and then
mill around until some of them are forced over.
As soon as one of them has seen the other side and
is evidently not frightened at what he sees, the
others take it for granted that everything is all
right.   This same distrust of the unseen and
unknown comes out again when sheep are being
handled at night.   Everything seems to frighten
them then, and it is hard to do anything with
them.

Perhaps the most distinctive characteristic
of sheep is their herd instinct.   What one does,
the rest are willing to take a chance on.   No
matter how hard the herder has to work to start
the sheep across a creek, if he can get a few or

even one to cross voluntarily, his troubles are
over. Where one goes, they all go. Sheep
handlers in the feed yards make good use of this
trait by having a pet sheep help them load the
cars. They lead the pet up the runway into
the car, and the rest make little difficulty about
following; when the car is full, they bring the
pet out again.

This herd instinct shows in a ludicrous way
when for any reason the bunch splits. Obviously the final split, the severing of the last link
as it were, must come between two sheep. It
is comical to see the ewe next to the break trying
to make up her mind which bunch to follow.
She does n't wish to part from either, and she
may make half a dozen false starts in either direction before she finally decides.

Sheep have the same liking for ice that the
Devil is supposed to have for holy water. A
sheep really stands upon eight points of horn,
and his weight is so slight in proportion to that
of other hoofed animals that he is practically
helpless on glare ice, a fact which he knows very
well. A frozen creek bare of snow will hold a
bunch of sheep almost as well as a woven-wire
fence, especially at the beginning of winter when
they have not seen ice for a long time. When
the herder wants the sheep to cross ice, he

either throws snow on it, or, better still, scatters a little dirt or sand across it.   Even a little of the latter serves to give the sheep a footing.

A fight between two ewes is a ludicrous sight. A falling out of some kind occurs between a couple of them, and the deadly conflict is on. The first thing they do is to lay back their ears till they look like a couple of snakes.   Then they take a few steps towards each other, walking stiff-legged, and when their heads are only a few inches apart they butt them together without force enough to jar loose a single idea. They repeat this two or three times, and the terrible fight is over.   I once saw two ewes that had had a prolonged argument and so had been left behind by the bunch.   Neither one wanted to be the first to run after it.   Finally one of them made the break, and was immediately hit in the rear by the other one.   Of course this caused another argument, and this time it was the other who went first and received a dose of her own medicine.   And so they alternated all the way to the bunch.

But if a fight between ewes is a joke, a fight between bucks is anything but.   They mean business and strive to inflict damage.   Contrary to what you would expect, the worst of the fighting does not take place in breeding time, but

in the off season. Perhaps it is because they
have nothing to think about then but fighting.
The two fighters back off a considerable distance
and come together head-on at full speed, and
their horns make a crack like a rifle shot.
Several times they may run together like that,
until one of them has had enough and runs
away from instead of at his foe. But occasionally they fight until one is so seriously injured
that death results. Consequently I always stop
the fight if I am near by. I used to say to my
dog, "Break it up! Jack, break it up!" and
he would streak it to the scene of the fight, nail
the nearest buck by the flank, and put an uncere-
monious and immediate stop to the proceedings.
After a while he did n't need to be told to "break
it up," but would be off as soon as he heard the
crack of the bucks' horns. And he grew so
fond of this police duty that he would n't even
let two ewes look cross at each other while he
was around, but, like the Irishman, he broke
up the riot before it began.

I saw one buck fight that had an unexpected
finish. The two bucks were fighting on a narrow
strip of level ground that had a twelve-foot cutbank on one side of it. As they backed away
from each other to get the proper distance, one
of them backed over the cutbank. When the

other buck saw his opponent suddenly vanish, he wheeled and made for the bunch as if the witches were after him. As for the one that went over the cutbank, he had the fight completely taken out of him. He turned one and a half somersaults and landed in a deep snowdrift. He remained there for some time in a sitting posture, apparently thinking things over, and then climbed out and made his way back to the bunch.

One of the most curious phenomena that is to be seen around a bunch of sheep is the kind of track that they occasionally make in the snow. Supposing the bunch has been grazing at a distance from the ranch all day. About four or five o'clock they begin to string in. The first sheep will always go single file, but as the front of the line has to break trail, and consequently goes slowly, more and more of the rear ones catch up to them, and presently instead of going single file there will be a thick column of sheep. When they have passed, it will often be noted that there are ridges of snow crossing their trail at right angles, giving the exact appearance of a corduroy road. These ridges are frequently ten or twenty feet long and usually as straight as if drawn with a ruler. The only explanation I have ever been able to think of for them is that every sheep uses the footsteps of the first sheep, and as they gradually break down the sides of the prints, they turn the original prints into trenches. But why they should break down the sides and not the front or back of the individual sheep track, I cannot see. Any other animal would be as likely to overlap the footprints forward or back as they would to the side.

It is often difficult to follow the processes of a sheep's mind. I once saw a ewe in a very small lamb bunch looking for her lamb. There were four white lambs in the bunch and one black one; hers was a black one. You would think that even a police detective could solve that problem without succumbing to brain fatigue. But no, she smelled of all the white lambs first and then of the black one. As soon as she sniffed of him she was satisfied.

This might seem to argue that sheep are color blind, but there is evidence to show that they are not. They pay much more attention to a black dog than they do to a lighter-colored one. Oftentimes when a black ewe is coming through the tall grass and is therefore indistinct, the sheep in front of her mistake her for the dog and begin to run. This of course startles the black sheep, and she runs after them as fast as she can. The others, now sure that she is the dog, run all the harder, and the chase continues until the sheep ahead scatter and swing to both sides where they can get a good look at what is chasing them.

When a ewe wishes to express defiance, she stamps her forefoot and sometimes she snorts. If she wishes to express further disapproval, say, of the presence of the dog, she walks away with her head held as high as possible, neck rigid and at right angles to her backbone.   In fact, an old ewe, with her neck as stiff as a ramrod and her feet mincing along as if she were treading on eggs, can express more outraged dignity than an old maid leaving a traveling man's experience meeting.

When a ewe shakes herself, she makes a thorough and complete job of it.   First she shakes her body, then she holds that still and shakes her head so fast that it becomes an indistinct blur like an electric fan.   The sound a sheep makes in shaking herself has the same tone quality as thunder; so that after a rain, if you shut your eyes, you cannot tell whether a given sound is a distant mutter of thunder or a near-by ewe shaking herself.

Speaking of noises, I think a sheep can make more different kinds than any animal that lives. They cough, they strangle, they gargle, they wheeze; they make a noise like a three-weeks-old baby choking to death on spaghetti; and once in a while you will hear some old ewe releasing a whole series of the most uncanny and ungodly noises, and you feel sure that she is in the very pangs of dissolution and trying to tell somebody where the money is hid. I have been with sheep a good many years, and every now and again I hear some noise that I never remember having heard before.

A ewe is a good mother according to her lights. She is continually losing track of her lamb, but she always finds him again. One of the prettiest sights I know of is to be seen every evening while the lambs are small. The ewes come in to the bed ground while the lambs in squads and shoals play along the cutbanks until they are tired. Then each lamb hunts up his mother and gets his evening meal. One by one the ewes lie down, and close beside each of them is curled her little lamb, mother and lamb chewing the cud of contentment with half-closed eyes, and over everything there is peace.

Ever since the first two social-minded cavemen agreed to live peaceably side by side and refrain from breaking each other's heads in order that they might the more safely and expeditiously cave in the head of any intruding caveman — ever since those early days we have had town life and country life. And ever since then we have been trying to change ourselves and our surroundings into something that perhaps they and we were never intended to be. Thousands of us hurl ourselves into cities like nuts into a hopper, and there by grinding and rubbing against one another we lose our natural form and acquire a superficial polish and a more or less standardized appearance. In the country the nuts (the pun, if any, is unintentional) are not subjected to this grinding process, at least to nothing like so great a degree. So if you want to find human nature "as is," in the original package and with the seals unbroken, never look for it in the city, where the younger generation tries to look as much as possible like the reigning movie actor or actress, as the case may be, and where the elder generation tries to be younger than their offspring, but go to the country, where the older generation is content to be itself, and where the younger generation either does not have the passion for standardization or lacks the means for attaining it.

The proof of this lies in your own experience. Any stenographer or "hello" girl can point out a thousand straphangers and subway mashers who look alike, dress alike, act alike, and pre-

sumably think alike. Whereas the countryside
knows that when Nature formed Amos G.
Ploughman, she broke the mould and will never
make another exactly like him. Friend and
foe may regard this with regret or relief, as the
case may be, but both accept the fact. By the
force of environment, by having to rely on
himself for a multitude of services, by his contin-
ual fight against enemies, both entomological
and political, the farmer of necessity becomes
self-reliant and independent. If ever there was
a farmer who thought that any other farmer
farmed just right, he has at least not yet been
caught and placed on exhibition. As the world's
champion all-round individualist, the farmer
wins the international sweepstakes.

Go a step further and you come to the solitary
worker, such as the lighthouse keeper, the fire
guard, and the herder. Here you find a man
who does not have the farmer's independence
of action, because his work is prescribed for him,
but who has more than the farmer's independence of character. That is, there are still fewer
external forces at work shaping his behavior,
and the internal forces have more play. There
are fewer contacts to knock off the rough edges
of his disposition, and there is more opportunity
for the full development of whatever is inherent

in the man. At the extreme end of this line would be the hermit, who is not only a law unto himself, but his own entire universe. The herder, thank heaven, stops far short of this. He is, however, like other solitary workers, apt to be introspective, sensitive to outside contacts when they come, and he broods over trifles that a man in a normal life would quickly forget. Like the farmer and the city man, he is the product of his environment.

But this is not to say that he is freakish-looking. A woman from the East visiting a sheep ranch made the remark that she would like to see what a herder looked like. So the next time the boss sent supplies to the wagon, he made arrangements for his visitor to go along. When she returned, he said, "Well, did you find out what a herder looked like?" "Why, yes," was the surprised answer. "He looks just like anybody else."

Granting then, for the sake of argument, that the herder is a human being, it remains to be seen in what particular ways his occupation affects him. And no sooner has that question been put than a host of people volunteer information, or what they fondly believe is such. Allusion has already been made to the most common slander on the herding profession — namely, that no one can herd for any length of time without losing his mental equilibrium, always supposing that he had it to start with. Almost anyone will admit that the herder, as the official chaperon for fifteen hundred strong-minded but misguided females, has a perfectly valid excuse for going crazy at any moment he may elect. However, I never knew one of them to avail himself of this privilege, and I never heard of an authentic case of its being done. But I have heard of several large institutions scattered throughout the land filled with interesting people who imagine that they are Confucius or Queen Marie or that the Prohibition law can be enforced (they always put cases of this kind in a padded cell), and there is no proof that any of these people ever so much as saw a sheep wagon.

But there are slanders worse than this; so bad, in fact, that they cannot be alluded to, other than to say that if they were true the herders would soon be enjoying the hospitality of their various state penitentiaries instead of sheep wagons.

Another libel is to the effect that the omnipresent bleating of the sheep combined with the total absence of human speech so works on the herder's very limited intelligence that he soon forgets human speech entirely and adopts instead the language of his charges.   In proof of this there is told the story of the traveling man who took a seat in a crowded train beside an old sheep herder, and by way of breaking the conversational ice asked him where he was from. "Montanaa-aa-aa-aa," replied the herder with the general intonation of a ewe calling her long-lost lamb.   "Where are you going?" was the next question.   "Baa-aa-aack," bleated the herder, and the traveling man, hastily pulling down his trousers to cover his wool socks, sought a seat in another car.

Then there was the herder who fell foul of the law, and since it was an open and shut case his lawyer advised him that his only chance lay in feigning a touch of herder's complaint and answering every question with a plaintive blat.   Like a wise client the herder followed his lawyer's instructions, and was forthwith discharged as incompetent, irresponsible, and a total intellectual loss.   Outside in the corridor his lawyer congratulated him on beating the case and then said, "Now how about my fee?" "Baa-aa-aa," answered the herder.

There is no denying, however, that the sheep do blat.   From lambing time until weaning the blatting is more or less continuous.   Lambs are forever getting lost and found. But when the bunch is rounded up to be driven somewhere, and hundreds of lambs are temporarily separated from their mothers, the noise is deafening. Take a thousand ewes, each convinced that she has seen the last of Little Woolly unless she can make her voice heard above the other nine hundred and ninety-nine, and a thousand lambs, each trying to locate his next hot meal by the same method, and the resulting uproar would make the proverbial boiler factory seem like an old ladies' home on a Sunday afternoon.

A herder gets accustomed to this noise, and pays no more attention to it than an engineer does to the roar of his train. To me the lowing of cattle and the blatting of calves is infinitely more annoying. At the ranch we had a milk cow that had a strong but misplaced affection for her brockle-faced calf, and a rich contralto voice to tell the world about it. In the natural course of events the calf was taken from her and shut up, and for days she never went very far from the barn. She would be grazing out a little way and all of a sudden she would remember that she had n't heard from her calf for at least twenty minutes, so she would let out a tentative bellow in the general direction of the barn. The calf would answer in moving tones, and the cow would start slowly towards the barn. More interchanges, and the cow would break into a gentle run. The closer she got, the more agonizing the appeals, and soon she would be rocking along, tail in air, bawling at every jump. Arrived at the barn, she and the calf would pour out their hearts and lungs to each other through a half inch of white pine, and the boss would have to talk to the hired man in the sign language until this heart-rending and ear-splitting duet was over.

Someone has suggested the possibility of having women sheep herders. Of course this must be a matter of deep concern to those men who earn their living in this profession, because it would seem that there ought to be one or two occupations at least to which man could retreat without the fear of being displaced by the weaker vessel.   Therefore it is not, I think, out of place to point out certain reasons why they ought not to be seriously considered in this connection. The truth is that in many respects they are un-suited to the work. With no more than a dis-creet allusion to the three quickest means of communication, can you really picture a woman engaging in an occupation which would leave her more or less in the dark with regard to the doings of even her immediate neighbors ?   And

of what use would it be to her to whisper a
dead secret into the fuzzy ear of a sheep, when
she knew that the recipient was physically inca-
pable of passing that secret on to where it would
do the most good ? Besides, the love affairs of
the sheep are all carried on with the greatest
openness, and there is no room for speculation,
innuendo, or scandal. Then, too, it is well
known that the favorite animal of a woman is a
cat, but it would be next to impossible to train
a cat to herd sheep, whereas a dog takes to it by
nature. Of course it might be possible to train
sheep to be herded by cats, but only a woman
would approach the problem from that end.

Then in the matter of vocabulary women
would be very seriously handicapped. There
are frequent occasions in herding when the feelings seethe in the herder's bosom like white-hot
steam in an engine boiler. His anguish finds
vent in language that he has picked up at odd
times around garages, stables, poker games, and
from autoists who were changing tires. Women,
not having frequented these places, would be at
a distinct disadvantage. A "pshaw," a "tut,"
even a "My goodness !" would be as inadequate
to the situation as a phony quarter would be to
apply on the national debt. It is said that a
woman finds relief in slamming doors and break-

ing things, but here again she would be at a disadvantage. Away out on the prairie, with the dog, or cat, keeping at a respectful distance, the only relief she would have would be to sit down and break into tears.

Then, too, the presence of a strange woman at the ranch leads to complications. We had a married couple working at the ranch last spring, and one day when I came in late to dinner and the hired man's wife and I were alone in the house, she started to go into a faint, and it was no feint either. As I saw her swaying and about to fall, the natural impulse was to place a brotherly arm about her slender waist and murmur reassuring phrases into her ear. But just as I was about to do so, I recalled having heard her husband saying only a few days before that if he ever caught any man fooling with his wife, he would shoot the variegated son of a sufficiently described ancestor and laugh at him while he was dying. Now it would be bad enough to be shot under a misapprehension, but to be laughed at while dying would be simply unbearable. So I withheld my arm and gave her my moral support only.

Herders, like workers in other lines, vary in the excellence of their work. There are careless herders and careful ones; there are lazy herders and, contrary to belief, there are industrious ones. The best of them will lose a sheep now and then, and the worst of them don't last long. I have heard of men who herded sheep for a whole year and never lost one. I have also heard of the sea serpent, the mermaid, and the unicorn. I am prepared to believe in any and all of them — when I see them.

X

THE HERDER'S NEIGHBORS

"A SHEEPMAN ain't got no friends" is the customary complaint of the flock owner. To this the classic retort is, "A sheepman don't want no friends." In other words, the farther away a sheepman's neighbors are, the more grass he has for his stock. Besides, it is often easier to be on good terms with someone at a distance whose interests do not in any way conflict with yours than it is with your neighbor whose lands may join yours for miles. If distance alone is enough to make friends, we all ought to be friendly in this part of the country where the population is less than two to the square mile and where, in spite of the one crop that never fails, there are fewer people than there were ten years ago. The ranch on which I work, one of average size, comprises about nineteen square miles, which would seem to give plenty of elbow room. Size, however, is only relative. Several years ago the boss was talking with the representative of a sheep company out in Montana. This man said that they had been dried out the previous year and had run short of range, and so had had to lease six additional townships. A township is thirty-six square miles.

A herder's neighbors fall into two distinct classes. First, there are those whose land borders his employer's range. It is the herder's business to see that the sheep do not cross the line separating the ranges, and the diligence with which he does this is in direct proportion to the irascibility of the said neighbors. The herder is brought into direct contact with each of these neighbors in turn during the course of a year, and these contacts are of varying pleasantness. The following, however, may almost be considered axiomatic : if the herder can convince the neighbors that he is trying to do the right thing, they, being human themselves, will overlook his occasional lapses from his 100 per cent ambitions. Besides this, they know that no herder can get the grass on his side up to the line without some of the sheep getting across; and if the neighbors themselves have stock running loose, as most of them do, they more than get that grass back again. Loose stock of any kind has very hazy ideas about boundary lines, but quite a clear conception of where the best feed is.

Of the many current sayings which we accept without examining them, one of the most foolish is that "it takes two to make a quarrel." As a matter of fact, any one person, if so disposed, can create an intolerable situation, in which his neighbors have the open and shut choice of surrendering their rights or maintaining them. But fortunately those who are disposed to create such a situation are few.

Sometimes a herder's difficulties are the fault of the sheepman. A new herder beginning work on a certain ranch asked his boss where the lines were. "Oh!" said the sheepman, making large and expansive gestures, "herd anywhere you like. It's all my range." The trustful herder set out with the sheep, but every time he crossed a boundary line someone popped up, and if he was n't the owner, then the land belonged to his brother or his aunt or his grandmother, and he had been especially commissioned to keep any and all sheep off it. That night the new herder tendered his resignation, to take effect at once.

Sometimes the shoe is on the other foot. A certain sheepman, hiring a herder with a reputation for quarrelsomeness, warned him before he went out to the wagon to begin work, "You can get into all the fights you want to, and you can get out of them yourself."

It is a curious fact that when the country was full of homesteaders, the hardest person to herd next to would be some old maid with just as many cattle and horses as she had children, and with the same likelihood of possessing any in the future. With the courage and tenacity of a crusader she would defend the grass, for which she had no possible use, against any and all comers. With the free and open hospitality of homestead days she might invite the herder to dinner, if he happened to be close by, but he would be expected to put in his time between courses chasing his sheep across the line.

The other class of neighbors with whom the herder has to do is comprised of people passing through the country on their various errands, or riders from other ranches looking for stock, or friends of the herder from a distance. The herder's relations with this class are uniformly pleasant.   Naturally if these men were not on friendly terms with the herder, they would not stop to pass the time of day with him or visit him at the wagon.   The herder is glad to see them.   They break the monotony of the herding day and, in a land without telephone or telegraph, they bring the latest news, and the herder is often able to reciprocate with news from other sources.   In fact, my boss used to say that the herder out on the prairie heard more news than he did at the ranch.   Scarcely a day goes by that the herder does not see someone.   The longest period I ever passed without seeing a human being was six days.   At the end of that time I was ready to marry or swear eternal brotherhood to the next person I met, according to sex. The absence of human companionship likewise has a tendency to make the tongue wag when the opportunity does come, for conversation with the sheep, however lively and vigorous it may be, is too one-sided to be interesting.

Yet, strange as it may seem, the herder sometimes has too much company and finds himself in the position of being the unpaid proprietor of a short-order stand.   Friends from a distance are always welcome, as their motives are above suspicion.   But when a near neighbor makes a practice of dropping in just at mealtime, a faint suspicion is apt to arise in the mind of the herder that his visitor is not so much attracted by the charm of the host's conversation as repelled by the thought of having to cook his own dinner at home. Whereupon a repulsion arises also in the mind of the herder, even to the point of wishing that he might slip a little arsenic into the coffee.

But it stands the herder in good stead not to antagonize his neighbors, whether near or far, because he never knows when they may be in a position to do him a most substantial favor. Once in a while a few sheep may slip away without the herder's knowledge, and a neighbor who will bring them back to the herder or tell him where they are confers a benefit worth many meals to the herder, and incidentally to the boss who pays for the food.

The transient rider going through the country and stopping at the wagon in the absence of the herder presents another problem. I have heard other herders say, and I take the same position myself, that if a man passing through is really in need of a meal, he is welcome to go into the wagon, cook himself a meal, wash his dishes, and go on, leaving the wagon in as good order as he found it. But that is just what the transient is unwilling to do. He will take liberties in a

sheep wagon that he would never dream of taking
in a private house, unless he had a friend along
to pick the buckshot out of him.   He will eat
up whatever food is cooked, especially any
delicacies, drain the coffee pot, and be on his
way rejoicing before the herder returns.   And
this man who eats up all the herder's cooked stuff
and leaves a pile of dirty dishes as a calling card
the herder would consign most heartily to a certain famous place once visited by the poet
Dante, but to a point in it several circles lower
than that brave man penetrated.

If the average herder were to write a book on
"Wild Animals I Have Known," he would
probably deal mainly with the jack rabbit, the
coyote, the rattlesnake, and the eagle.   Of course
there is plenty of other wild life in this land

> Where the wind never ceases,
> And the flea never dies,

but some of it is beneath contempt and some
of it is common to the rest of the country also.
But the animals named above are for the most
part peculiar to the far West.
    The herder has, of course, no scientific knowl-
edge of these animals.   He does n't know the
scientific names of any of them.   But to compen-
sate for this he has a lot of pet English names for

them that are more descriptive than the Latin ones. All of the animals named above cross his path frequently, and two of them are of intimate concern to him.

The commonest of these animals is the jack rabbit. In fact he is so common that sometimes he gets to be an unmitigated nuisance. Then rabbit hunts are organized, and on certain appointed days everybody with an old gun and a good eye turns out. The hunters are divided into two sides by lot, and the side bagging the most rabbits is treated to an oyster supper by the losers, who of course help eat it.

The jack rabbit is much larger than the Eastern rabbit. It is brown in summer and white in winter. It travels in great leaps, and when going its best can jump incredible distances. It has long, powerful hind legs and short front ones, like a kangaroo. This places it at a disadvantage when going downhill; therefore it always heads uphill when being chased, which in turn puts the dog at a disadvantage. A jack rabbit will make a fool of any ordinary dog, both for speed and for endurance. Any canine, whether hound or otherwise, that can overhaul and pull down a jack in a fair straightaway race is all dog. And yet there are dubs of dogs that will chase any rabbit they sight, although they have never come within smelling distance of one yet.

The rabbit may be either a source of annoyance or of pleasure to the herder. If he has a rabbit-chasing dog, he has to be continually on his guard for fear the dog will jump one, chase it, and tie the sheep up in a knot. On the other hand, if the herder carries a .22, the jack rabbit will solve his problem of dog meat. Although the jack has well-deserved confidence in his speed, he also relies a good deal on his power of concealment, and as long as he thinks himself unobserved it is possible to approach him close enough for an easy shot.

The jack rabbit has a cousin, the cottontail rabbit, which is much smaller and is brown both winter and summer. He is also at all seasons of the year a most toothsome morsel. When rolled in corn meal and fried in butter till there is a brown crust over him, he is warranted to make a vegetarian suffer total amnesia of the principles.

But if the herder regards the jack rabbit with mixed feelings, he has only one feeling for the coyote, and that is an undying hatred. He regards him as his arch enemy, as an unmitigated pest, and as a blot on the face of Nature. Someone has called the coyote the comedian

of the plains, but that person either never saw
a lamb after a coyote was through with it or
else he had a very peculiar sense of humor.
The coyote, too small to command respect, like
the larger killers, and too smart to be easily
trapped or poisoned, remains the herder's night-
mare and the sheepman's bogey. He has infinite cunning, no inconvenient courage, is quite
prolific, and in the face of universal detestation
has managed not only to maintain himself in his
old territories, but to extend them, so that he is
no longer confined to the prairie states, but has
spread eastward to the Mississippi and north-
ward far into Canada.

The coyote is of reddish-gray color and about
the size of a large collie. Some collies look much
like coyotes. The coyote, however, has a bushy
tail like a fox, and a long pointed nose and
pointed ears. His favorite food is anything he
can chew, and when he is eating meat he is not
at all particular about the date of its decease.
While a wolf almost always makes his own kill
and eats it fresh, a coyote will pick up a rabbit
or rob a bird's nest or feed on an ancient and
full-flavored carcass with equal relish.

With all this broad-mindedness in regard to
food, it would seem an easy matter to poison a
coyote. But part of his protection is his devil-

ish cunning, which not only makes him the hardest animal to trap there is, but makes him very suspicious of meat offerings too conveniently placed.   Another objection to the use of poison is that it kills so many dogs as to create a sentiment against its use — that is, among people whose stock is not troubled by coyotes.   The poison bait may or may not tempt the suspicious coyote, but it is sure death to any unsuspecting dog that passes that way.   Even at that, poisoning has proven the most effective method of keeping the coyote in check.   The rosiest optimist does not consider the possibility of his extermination.

A certain Metropolitan opera singer once made the statement that she thought it cruel to trap even destructive wild animals, but believed they ought to be brought together in one place and securely fenced in.   If she had gone one step further and explained how this might be done, she would never have had to sing another note. Her remark is merely one more example of that maudlin perversion that has every sympathy for the criminal and none whatever for the victim.

Speaking of singing, the most distinctive characteristic of the coyote is his song.   It consists of a series of sharp staccato barks, merging into a long and dying wail.   It is

usually heard at night, for that is the time of
the coyote's activity. The peculiar thing about
it is that when two coyotes are singing a duet,
as they are very fond of doing, they do not bark
haphazardly or in unison, but they catch each
other up with lightning-like quickness, so that
two coyotes will produce such a torrent of barks
that the uninitiated would swear there was a
large pack of them. On a cold winter's night you
will hear this two-piece orchestra tuning up on
some distant butte, and then miles away in
another direction you will hear an answering
chorus; then the cry will be picked up in still
other directions, until it seems as if the whole
landscape were tossing this weird melody up
toward the cold and unappreciative stars.

It is not to be supposed that the coyote has
been allowed to have his own way unchecked.
There have been two main lines of attack upon
him. First, various states have placed a bounty
on him, and the counties where he has been
particularly troublesome have added another.
In this county, for example, there was formerly
a total bounty of seven dollars a coyote, and the
hunters could still sell the skin. The other
method of attack is by the Federal Government
through the Biological Survey. This government bureau has trained men as hunters, put

them in the field, and gone after the coyotes with traps, guns, and poison.   The coyote that dines with the Biological Survey does n't need any supper.

There is a controversy on in this state at present over the respective merits of the bounty system and the hunger system.   To one who has herded under both systems, there can be little question.   Under the old bounty system the sheep could not be trusted out of sight, and losses by coyotes sometimes reached 10 per cent. Almost any night you could hear them howling from all points of the compass.   Now, after three or four years of systematic work by the hunters of the Biological Survey, it is rarely that you see a coyote, and their song is no longer flung so freely to the night breezes.   Incidentally, sheep losses have been cut to a fraction of what they were.

A moment's consideration will show why this is so.   Most of the opposition to the Federal system comes from disgruntled bounty hunters who would like to be able to slip a seven-dollar shell into their rifle every time they see a coyote. The bounty hunter works when he feels like it, and lays off when he pleases.   He does not hunt in summer when the fur is valueless, but waits till winter when he can get from ten to twenty dollars for a pelt in addition to the bounty. And even in winter he works only when the weather is good; on cold and stormy days he keeps the home fires burning, and who can blame him? But the crux of the matter is that the bounty hunter is not interested in the extermination of the coyote, but only the coyote as a source of profit. This was clearly shown by the action of one bounty hunter who offered a government man the scalp of a male coyote for every female he should turn loose from his traps.

On the other hand, we have in the hunters of the Biological Survey a body of trained men whose one aim is the total extermination of the coyote species. They work on a salary and are not interested in the value of the furs, so they are just as keen to get coyotes in summer as in winter. They work six days a week, in bad weather and good. They must obtain a certain minimum number of scalps every month, and if they fail to maintain this average they are dropped from the force. But if they regularly exceed this number, they receive additional rewards in honor and pay. Thus they have every incentive to exterminate the coyote, and none not to. Is it any wonder that they get results? Wolves were formerly a serious menace. In fact the Government estimates that while a

coyote does a hundred dollars' worth of damage a
year, a wolf kills one thousand dollars' worth of
stock in the same period. But so relentless has
the pursuit of them been that they have been
almost annihilated as far as the interior states
are concerned. They still trickle across the
border from Canada and Mexico and do some
damage before they are killed, but our own
Government is coöperating with the other two
to the end that not only shall these undesirable
aliens be excluded, but that they shall be destroyed if possible at their point of origin.

The porcupine, another animal that the herder
occasionally sees, presents two separate problems,
one in economics and one in natural history.
To consider the last first, what delirious joy does
a dog derive from biting a porcupine that leads
him to make a canine pincushion of himself
every time he sees one ? You would think that
one experience of having the barbed quills pulled
out or pushed through would be entirely sufficient. But apparently not. Still, we must
not judge the dog too harshly. There are men
who will bite on every oil proposition they see,
and get just as badly stuck too.

Like the rest of us, the porcupine is sometimes
the beneficiary and sometimes the victim of economic law. In the Canadian woods he is rigor-

ously protected, because of the economic value of his flesh to the hypothetical lost wanderer, this value being vastly greater than that of the trees he destroys.   In other words, Canada is long on trees, but short on meat that can be secured with no other weapon than a club.   But on the almost treeless prairies the conditions are reversed. In the first place it is unlikely that anyone will get lost in a region where he can see most of the surrounding four states by climbing only a moderately high hill.   So the economic value of the porcupine in these regions is very much less than the value of the trees that must succumb to his bark-eating proclivities.   Hence he finds himself on the list of the proscribed. If the porcupine would only betake himself from the place where he is an economic liability to a place where he would be an economic asset, he would have more of a chance to transmit his general dumbness to posterity.   For in any intelligence test the porcupine could not possibly rate higher than minus zero, and even this mark would be a compliment to his mental attainments.

We use certain standard similes, drawn from the animal kingdom, to express certain attributes of mankind.   We say that a man is as brave as a lion, or as hungry as a bear.   When we wish

to convey the idea that a man is sneaky or under-
handed, we say that he is a snake in the grass.
If we should call a man a rattlesnake, we should
probably think we had plumbed the nadir of
meanness and treachery; and yet, judged by
all the standards that we use in judging one
another, the rattlesnake is a gentleman.

In the first place, he is never the aggressor.
All he asks is to be allowed to attend to his own
business. Furthermore, if he is disturbed, he
will even stretch a point and will peaceably with-
draw if allowed to do so. He never strikes without warning, if he has time to warn. He will
begin rattling at the approach of a disturber,
and he will keep on rattling as long as that person is in the vicinity. If he is cornered and
believes himself in danger, he will strike with
the best weapon he has, and you or I would do
the same. His rattle is at first only a warning.
If angered, he will no longer try to crawl away,
but will remain coiled until the issue is decided.
When the stones begin to drop on him, he will
try to protect his head with some of his coils,
but he will rattle defiance to the last; a fair
fighter and a brave one.

People have an exaggerated idea of the deadli-
ness of a rattler's poison. A relatively small
proportion of those that are bitten die; but

the consequences are in any case so painful and serious that a snake's rattle, if heard by human ears, is usually the equivalent of his death rattle. The snake is easy to kill — stones, old bones, a bridle, or a lariat rope being the common tools of destruction. I have known old-timers who would wait till the snake was crawling away, turn him over with the toe of their boot, and then tramp on his head before he had time to right himself. But that is a form of gambling that never appealed to me. I knew one plucky little schoolma'am from Wisconsin who killed a nine-rattle snake with her umbrella. Once, for lack of other ammunition, I hit a rattler with an unabridged edition of Shakespeare. The snake was never the same again, but neither was Shakespeare.

If you examine the cases of those who have been bitten, you will find that in most of them the victim stepped on or near the snake before the latter was aware of his presence. Thus a little girl in this county, getting off her horse to open a gate, stepped squarely on a rattler and was bitten in the leg. That leg never grew, but always remained shrunken. While the snake is almost never the aggressor, its means of defense is so powerful that it cannot be tolerated. It is a victim of its own efficiency.

It is an old saying that you might as well kill a man as scare him to death. It so happens that there are several good imitations of the sound of a snake's rattle. There is a weed in this region whose dry pods, when carelessly kicked in walking, give off a sound almost like a snake on the warpath, enough like it anyway to induce a gentle perspiration in a man who has recently killed a rattler or seen one. For a day or two after an encounter with a snake you see and hear them everywhere, even without the aid of the forbidden juice. Then there are certain insects whose sudden buzzing somewhat resembles that of a snake. There was even a lamb several years ago whose rasping blat many a time caused me to jump. But although there are several sounds that may be mistaken for a snake's rattle, the genuine one is never mistaken for anything else. The few seconds between the time when you hear the snake rattle and the time when you locate him are extremely unpleasant ones. He may be two or three yards away and he may be right beside you. Your first impulse is to do a standing broad jump, but the wiser plan is to locate the snake first, so that you may jump intelligently.

The rattlesnake has certain likes and dislikes. He is apt to be found on stony hillsides and along cutbanks, but actually he may be encountered anywhere. He likes warmth, in spite of his being a cold-blooded animal, and he will often crawl under a coat or blanket lying on the ground. He has also been known to crawl into the beds of people sleeping on the ground. Therefore some people who object to sharing their bed with a snake refuse to sleep on the ground at all.

Many people think of a rattlesnake as coiled round and round like a garden hose, and as striking from that position. But the fact is that only the last half or third of the snake is so coiled when it is in the striking position. The rest is looped back and forth in a series of *S*'s, and it is the sudden straightening out of these *S*'s that constitutes the strike of the snake. He does not jump, because it is the coil or two left on the ground that gives him the leverage for the blow. A young fellow once told me of how a snake struck at him from the top of a bank and whizzed right past his ear. But I think that that particular snake lay coiled in the bottom of a jug, and animals of that sort have been known to do some very remarkable things.

Human beings are not the only sufferers from the rattlesnake. Colts especially seem prone to be bitten. A colt has a large bump of curiosity.

He wants to find out what that queer buzzing thing is, and he puts his nose closer and closer until the inevitable strike comes. If he survives, he carries a balloon-shaped head around with him for some time. The fact that some horses have a terror of rattlers, while others are indifferent to them, may point to some such early experience.

To my mind Nature's noblest representatives in this part of the world are the great bald-headed and golden eagles that perch on rocky pinnacles or float in lazy circles under the very vault of heaven. Storms mean nothing to an eagle. I have seen one sitting on a point of rock while a blizzard was raging past him and driving all other creatures before it into shelter. There seems to be a natural dignity in his posture and the turn of his head, and a nobility in his curved beak and flashing eye. Once, as I lay on a rocky hilltop, an eagle swooped within a few feet of me, saw me, and wheeled, and as the sun struck his back it was burnished gold from wing tip to wing tip.

Sometimes the fear is expressed that our wild life is doomed. As for the animals I have mentioned, the jack rabbit is omnipresent and prolific. He knows his multiplication table too well not to survive. The coyote, pest as he is, has proven his ability to keep a foothold even where every man's hand is against him. The fact that we find the rattlesnake in Virginia and Florida, settled for hundreds of years, indicates that he will survive. The eagle, nesting in inaccessible places, and floating serenely far above the earth, would seem to be able to fend for himself.

It really seems too bad that we can't turn the attention of our myriads of hunters to the killing off of destructive species instead of the harmless and beautiful ones. As things stand, the city sportsman puts on seventy-five dollars' worth of hunting toggery, fills his shotgun half full of assorted slugs, goes out and knocks over a couple of song birds, and calls it a day. Think how much more valuable these slugs would be in the innards of a coyote or even a skunk. But that would have the deadly defect of being useful, and therefore not sport. Then there are our great hunt clubs. It is a curious commentary on human nature that, whereas the country dweller can go out into the woods and bag his game without so much as changing his hat, when a city man goes hunting he has to wear a peculiar garb, and when society turns out en masse to rid the earth of a dangerous fox or a ferocious rabbit, it decks itself out like a three-ring circus. Now if the hunt clubs, instead of chasing rabbits or foxes raised for the purpose, should be minded to come to the aid of the Western stockman, they could accomplish their laudable purpose in one of two ways : it might well be that one glimpse of the hunt, with its extraordinary costumes, its strange behavior, and its outlandish cries, would so frighten the wild denizens of the territory that they would flee this part of the country never to return ; or it might be that the coyote, being one of the wisest of animals, would try to figure out why any adult human being should dress and act like that, and the rash attempt to solve the unsolvable would inevitably bring on softening of the brain, and he would perish miserably.

It is significant of the fact that this is still a frontier country that the most famous product of Harding County should have been an outlaw. This, however, was no ordinary two-legged out-law with a killing or two to his credit, but a large gray wolf that for thirteen years laughed at poison, traps, and guns, lived in and off enemy country with the hand of every man against him — a cunning, bloodthirsty, and remorseless killer, a superwolf among wolves, and the most destructive single animal of which there is any record anywhere.

It seems impossible that an animal weighing only seventy-five pounds could attain to such an eminence. Yet, when in his prime, Three Toes, as he came to be called, did not hesitate to match his strength against any steer or full-grown horse. In his old age he confined himself principally to sheep, as being so much easier to kill, but this very facility in killing made him that much more destructive. Where other wolves reckoned the damage they did in thousands of dollars, Three Toes reckoned his in tens of thousands. From first to last he destroyed fifty thousand dollars' worth of stock that could be definitely laid to his charge. This does not take account of the many kills he must have made that were never discovered or that were attributed to other causes, but only those kills that were indisputably his own.

For first, last, and all the time, Three Toes was a killer. Other wolves might kill one cow or sheep and eat off that and be satisfied. But Three Toes killed for the sheer love of killing. He would kill on a full stomach as well as when hungry. On one occasion he visited three different ranches in one night, killed many sheep and lambs at each one, but ate only the liver of one lamb. At one of the ranches the lambs lay around the next morning as if they were sleeping ;

but the head or breast of each one was crushed. Three Toes' powerful jaws had crushed the bone, but his worn teeth had not penetrated the skin.   Right beside a scarecrow, put up to keep the coyotes away, three lambs lay piled criss-cross.   The sheepman said that it looked as if Three Toes were afraid his work would be over-looked.

There is a legend that this wolf was born in Montana, a supposition possibly based on the wildness of his subsequent career.   But the more generally accepted tradition is that he was whelped in the breaks along the Little Missouri River, about sixty miles south of Roosevelt's ranch on the same stream.   The year of his birth, of course, is unknown, but by 1912 he had emerged definitely as a killer.   By that time he had also sustained the injury that won him his nickname.   A toe on one of his forefeet had been pinched off in a trap, and the mark of this maimed foot he subsequently left in the dust of many a sheep corral, a print as legible and as damning as any fingerprint at police headquarters.   A man trapping wolves in that vicinity two years before had caught two wolves in one night and had found the toe of a third wolf in another trap.   He always believed that this belonged to Three Toes, and those who are interested in coincidences may find one in the fact that the last big kill of cattle made by Three Toes was in this man's herd.

Three factors contributed to Three Toes' long immunity from punishment — his endurance, his cunning, and his phenomenal luck. A certain rancher, an old-timer, who had run down many a wolf, declared that Three Toes was the fastest-running, longest-winded wolf he had ever seen, and time and again did Three Toes vindicate that judgment. At one time he had been killing stock for a certain family in the Cave Hills, and three or four of the sons decided to get rid of him. It happened that there was fresh light snow on the ground, which made it easy to track him. They jumped him early one morning, and the chase was on. The wolf first made a circle of about ten miles; and then, seeing that he had not shaken off his pursuers, he struck out for the Short Pine Hills, forty or fifty miles away. In the course of the day's ride the brothers stopped at a ranch house for dinner and there changed horses. When they took up the trail again, they saw the spot where the wolf had lain resting while they ate. Occasionally during the afternoon they caught glimpses of him, but always too far away for a shot. Once they saw the feet and ears of a jack rabbit alongside his trail, showing that he too had dined.   At dark, after having run him all of seventy miles that day, they stopped at a near-by ranch for the night.

In the morning when they took up the pursuit again, the wolf's tracks revealed how he had passed the night.   Less than a quarter of a mile from where they quit the chase, the wolf had lain down for several hours, evidently very tired. Then he had gone to the top of the highest hill in the vicinity and there had lain on guard until morning.   In fact he did not move until he saw them coming, since his tracks showed that he had left the hill on the run.   But the men had not followed very far before they were dumfounded to find that the tracks were swinging back toward their own ranch in the Cave Hills.   All that day they followed helplessly, and it was a very disgusted bunch of men that finally quit the tracks just about a mile from their own ranch house.

Two days later, with a fresh fall of snow, they took him for another run to the Short Pine Hills. But there the snow left them, and they were obliged to abandon the chase and return home. So did the wolf.   Four days later they jumped him again, and took him for a run of twenty-five miles.   Although he returned as before, he seemed to have acquired a vague suspicion that his company was n't wanted around there, for shortly after that he betook himself to a more restful neighborhood.

A Federal hunter, who spent nine fruitless months in pursuit of this one wolf, once ran him for three consecutive days. On one of these days he ran him ninety-five miles and changed saddle horses five times. At the end of the third day the snow disappeared, but by that time the hunter was convinced, as others had been before him, that it was impossible to run this wolf down. Another time, while Three Toes was being pursued by a man with a relay of saddle horses, he was so far in the lead that he took time to jump into a sheep corral and kill fifteen head.

In addition to his phenomenal endurance, the Harding County wolf had cunning to quite an unusual degree. He habitually slept or rested on the tops of the highest hills, so that he could command the surrounding country; or in niches on the sides of clay buttes, where his color made him almost invisible. He did practically all his hunting at night. Every attempt was made to poison him, but he consistently refused to pick up the baits. He needed no one to provide his meat for him. When being run by horsemen, he soon learned to make for rough country and to go under a fence whenever possible.

Several attempts were made to run him down with dogs. One man brought a pack of hounds into the country for that purpose, but when he heard tales of the wolf's ferocity he changed his mind, and would not allow his pack to be put on the trail. At another time a man was running the wolf with hounds and was pressing him close. The wolf when jumped had tried his usual method of leading through places difficult for horsemen and under fences, but he soon discovered that these offered no more difficulty to his pursuers than to himself. He then made straight for the banks of the Little Missouri River. Of course every inch of this territory was familiar to him, so it could not have been by chance that he struck the river at a point where there was a thirty-foot bank. Over this the wolf plunged fearlessly. The dogs refused the leap, and their quarry escaped.

Another time, again while running through familiar country, the wolf led the chase down the bed of a dry draw. At one point this draw was separated from the next one by only a thin curtain of earth about twelve feet high, some little distance above the junction of the two draws. When the wolf reached this point, he gave a mighty leap, cleared the partition wall without touching it, and backtracked up the other draw for dear life. Of course, as far as the dogs were concerned, he might as well have vanished into thin air.

Another remarkable thing about Three Toes was his unvarying luck. He always got the breaks of the game. At various times community hunts were organized to capture him. On the appointed day men would assemble from all directions, converging toward a point where they had good reason to believe he would be. But he was never there. On one of these days the wife of a former sheriff was going on horseback to a neighboring ranch, and she ran squarely on to him. He was crossing his pursuers' tracks diagonally, but behind them. The sheriff's wife was a good shot, but she had no gun with her. The wolf's luck still held. That night he killed one of the best saddle horses in the country.

There is a temptation to romanticize in writing about this wolf. And yet the unvarnished facts of his career are romantic enough. It has been estimated that upwards of a hundred and fifty men, not counting those in the organized hunts, tried at one time or another to win fame by capturing him. He was seen repeatedly, once within a mile of the county seat, but always by people without guns, or at too great a distance. Up to 1920 he was known to have a mate, but in that year she was captured, and from then on he played a lone hand. He always had a coyote or two as hangers-on. When one would be killed or trapped, another would take its place. Three Toes set a good table.

Another instance of this wolf's unfailing luck was when three Federal hunters jumped him unexpectedly. For one instant there was a chance for a standing shot; the next, their target was a swiftly moving streak through the tall grass, belly close to the ground. Eighteen shots were fired, but none of them took effect. It was not that the men were poor marksmen. All were good shots — one of them remarkably so.

Another time Three Toes was going down a cow path thickly set with traps in anticipation of his coming. He actually sprang one of the traps, but his large foot happened to rest on the jaw as well as on the pan, and, as the trap sprung, the jaw threw his foot clear.

But no pitcher can go to the well indefinitely, and Three Toes' career was drawing to a close. In 1923 he made his greatest kill for any one year, twelve thousand dollars' worth. Most sheep ranches have woven-wire enclosures to keep the

bucks in during the season when they must be
kept out of the main bunch. A coyote rarely
tackles a buck, having a wholesome respect for
his horns, so the buck pastures are considered
safe. But to a wolf well able to kill a full-grown
horse or steer, a buck is easy prey. Three Toes
killed in the buck pastures systematically and
enthusiastically, and as a pure-bred buck is worth
thirty dollars, it did not take him long to do considerable damage. While the average wolf or
coyote fears an enclosure of any kind, Three
Toes was absolutely fearless in this regard. His
first big kill of sheep occurred when he entered a
corral situated at a distance from the ranch
house and killed thirty-five head in one night.
On another occasion he approached a house
from which the family was temporarily absent,
and finding five bum lambs shut up in a pen
next to the house (they were shut up on account of him), he killed them all. Sheer, wanton butchery.

In the spring of 1925, Three Toes was slaugh-
tering at the rate of a thousand dollars a month.
The Board of County Commissioners decided
to increase the bounty on him to five hundred
dollars. But at the request of the head of the
Biological Survey in this State, they delayed
action till he should send out still another Federal

hunter. This man was Clyde F. Briggs, whose
specialty was the taking of gray wolves, and who
already had the scalps of several famous ones to
his credit.   He had carried on wolfing operations
in Arizona and other parts of the Southwest,
and in the Ozarks.   Briggs came out to Harding
County early in July bringing his traps and
equipment with him, and he made his headquarters at the ranch where the wolf had been
doing most of his recent killing.

The morning after his arrival, with the ground
soft from an overnight rain, the sheepman was
able to show him the tracks of the killer, where
he had emerged from a patch of bad lands.
Briggs took a match from his pocket and measured the track. "That wolf," he remarked as he
rose, "weighs about seventy-five pounds." As
a matter of fact the wolf tipped the scale at
seventy-four and a fraction. Briggs found by
inquiry that the wolf was in the habit of making periodic trips through this territory, and on
that fact he based his campaign. His plan was
simple. He would put traps along every trail
that the wolf would be likely to follow in entering
or leaving this region. But it was here that the
wolfer's special knowledge came in. Only a
wolfer could tell what trails a gray would be
likely to use. Briggs had heard many tales of

the uniqueness of Three Toes among wolves,
but after following his tracks for a short distance
he delivered himself of a second dogmatic statement: "That wolf is a gray wolf, and just like
all the other gray wolves." Briggs had the advantage over certain other dogmatists in seeing
his dogmas prove themselves to the hilt.

It would take too long to detail the infinite
pains that Briggs took in setting his traps. Suffice to say that, experienced as he was, it took
him about two hours to make one setting of two
traps; but when he was through, you could
stand within ten feet of his set and be utterly
unable to point to the place. The ground looked
just as it did before, yet lurking under the loose
dust were two pairs of steel jaws ready to fly
up and grasp with lightning quickness anything that touched the pan. Between the two
traps would be the sage bush on which he
sprinkled natural scent, — that is, urine taken
from other wolves, — which has proved itself
an irresistible lure to any wolf.

There were fourteen of these wolf sets, and
guarding each one were two coyote sets, one on
each side. The idea was that the wolf sets were
for the accommodation of Three Toes only, and
the coyote sets were for the purpose of keeping
the wolf sets undisturbed. The coyote sets

were baited with a very strong-smelling fish oil, so as to attract all the attention possible. The necessity for them was proven by the fact that in the fifteen days of the campaign they took three coyotes, three dogs, two badgers, two skunks, and numbers of jack rabbits and sage hens. Of course the wolf sets did not go scatheless, but they were protected to a great degree. Every day Briggs made the rounds of his traps in his car, relieving them of their unwanted victims, and resetting and rebaiting them. His daily round measured thirty-three miles.

There was one particular wolf set on which he had pinned his hopes, and the fourth night it caught something. But Three Toes' luck was still with him, and it was a coyote that paid the penalty for his curiosity. Three Toes came along that very trail later in the night, and he seemed to take a great interest in his substitute, for he made a complete circle around him before continuing on down the trail. Since this set was now useless for his purpose, Briggs transferred it to a low rise overlooking the Little Missouri River. There, beside an old road, he found an ideal location for a set, except that there was no sage bush on which to sprinkle the scent. Briggs remedied this by transplanting a bush to the desired spot.

For ten days Briggs made his daily rounds, rebaiting and resetting. Three Toes had temporarily left that part of the country and gone over into Montana, where he made a small kill, his last. On the morning of July 23 Briggs set out as usual, and had tended about half his traps when he approached the one with the transplanted bush. As he topped the rise and came in sight of it, he saw that his quest was ended. The great wolf lay stretched beside the trail, his head on his paws like a dog before the fire. As Briggs and his companion came toward him, he raised his head, but would not get to his feet.

Leaving his companion on guard, Briggs returned to the ranch to get his camera and spread the news. Everyone at the ranch accompanied him back. They tried again to induce the wolf to stand, but he refused. There had been a rain the night before, and the tracks told the whole story. The wolf had come from the west, stopped to smell of the bush, and in walking about had stepped into one of the traps with a forefoot. He had been in traps twice before, but had been caught by the toes only and had been able to pull free. This time, however, the jaws had gripped him high up on the leg. He had plunged about in his efforts to free himself and had stepped into the other trap with a hind foot, which also had been gripped high up. Even then he had struggled and torn up the ground till he was exhausted. Now he lay quiet, showing no fight, seemingly indifferent.

Briggs, working barehanded while the others stood at a respectful distance, put a wire muzzle over the wolf's jaws, and then the men lifted him into the back of Briggs's car. The traps were left on him for fear he might bleed to death. One of the men assured Briggs that he would be able to take him alive to Rapid City; but out of his experience with other wolves Briggs answered, "He won't live to see Buffalo."

They started for the ranch and had gone about three miles when one of the men called out, "Clyde! I believe that wolf is dying!" Briggs stopped the car and, looking around, found the wolf's eyes fixed on him. But the eyes did not see him, for the wolf was dead.

Call it a broken heart or what you will — something of this sort it was that killed the old wolf. He was resting easily when found, his injuries were superficial, and he had been handled with the greatest care. But there was something in his proud old spirit that could not brook captivity, and Nature, more merciful than he had ever been, granted him his release.

It was the custom in ancient Rome for a returning conqueror to exhibit his captives through the city streets. The old wolf was spared this humiliation, and yet he died in chains in the car of his conqueror with his eyes fixed on the one man who had ever been able to outwit him.

XI

READING AND OTHER AMUSEMENTS

If time were really money, the herders would soon exchange places with the multimillionaires, for the latter never have any time at all and the former have all there is. Even if a herder does not particularly care for reading, he will be driven to it in self-defense. What he reads will depend on his personal tastes and his opportunities for getting books and papers, but it is a safe bet that his first thought will be for his local paper.

Ever since some prehistoric editor ruined the whole face of a cliff getting out his Sunday edition, and shortly after that had his head broken with a stone club in the hands of some irate reader — ever since those early days editors have been a wary and therefore a long-lived race. It is one thing to call the prime minister of Bulgaria everything from a reactionary to a chicken thief, and quite another thing to intimate, however delicately, that the taste of Bud O'Bolger in girls and neckties might conceivably be improved. The prime minister of Bulgaria is a busy man and besides that may not have car fare at the time being, but Bud O'Bolger is right on the spot and apt to drop in almost any time to say, "Howdy do," and also, "How come?"

Besides this natural instinct for self-preservation, the editor, and especially the country editor, is further complicated by a very real bias in favor of democracy with a small *d*. Whatever his political leanings may be as expressed in upper-case letters, his devotion to small *d* democracy is usually patent throughout his paper, and especially in the personal items. The terms "hired man" and "hired girl," for example, are not to be found in his vocabulary.

Therefore the herder in perusing his local paper takes into consideration the two editorial qualities mentioned above and reads in the light of previous and contemporaneous knowledge, this

in turn to be amplified by subsequent knowledge.
Take, for example, the following item : —

> Mr. Latham Sleeper has severed his
> connection with the Bar X ranch.

The editor neglects to state that the severance
was entirely involuntary on Mr. Sleeper's part,
that it was preceded by a violent stoppage of
his pay and accompanied by a verbal blast
that rocked the English language on its founda-
tions. The editor probably knows all this, but
he does not mention it, and thereby Mr. Sleeper's
already lacerated feelings are saved any further
contusions.

Take another item : —

> Miss Bessie Dumplings has accepted an
> invitation to assist Mrs. Ranchman in the
> near future.

This does not mean that Mrs. Ranchman con-
templates giving a reception and desires to have
Miss Bessie's eye-filling figure next to hers in
the receiving line. No, Miss Bessie's social
duties will be confined to chaperoning the dishes
from the table to the cupboard via the dish pan,
and to accompanying the family laundry up and
down the washboard. Of course she will have
time off for any dances that happen along and
time out on the appearance of any eligible —
that is, any unattached male on the sunny side

of ninety-three. For although Mrs. Ranchman has made her kill under the one-buck law and has officially retired from the chase, still the inherited instincts of six thousand years cannot be stifled in an instant, and she welcomes the opportunity to do a little hunting by proxy. In this cruel pastime there is very little sportsmanship shown, and the game laws afford absolutely no protection, the last closed season having ended with the birth of Eve; since when man has put up a game but losing fight in the unequal battle of sex, where the odds are all on the other side.

This item also means that if at the aforesaid dances Mr. Ranchman presumes on his temporary official position in the matter of asking for dances, he is due to be severely snubbed. For the independence for which our fathers fought and died, and even the independence of a labor-union leader, is as nothing compared with the independence of a girl in a community where she is at a premium. Women have never been bearish on their charms, but where they conceive that anything like a corner in the market exists, the sky is the limit.

Many a city man looking over a country paper for the first time, and finding column after column devoted to the unimportant doings of presumably unimportant people, jumps to the conclusion that the editor is in this way tickling the vanity of his fellow citizens in the hope of building up his subscription list. But the city man is shooting wide of the mark. To be sure, country people like to see their names in the paper, — a weakness which they share with governors and presidents, — but the real reason the editor prints these items is that that is the news his subscribers want to read.

City people are interested in events, country people in each other. The city man wants to know the result of the ball game, but he neither knows nor wants to know anything about the family that lives next door to him, to the right hand or the left, or above or below him. As for the country dweller, organized baseball leaves him cold, as a rule, but he has a pretty good idea of what is happening to his neighbors for a radius of ten miles or so. The countryside, for instance, knows all about the row old man Smith had with his wife. They know what started it and what she said. The only thing they don't know is what he would have said if he had had a chance to say anything. But they can pretty nearly guess that anyway.

The city man has a disjointed knowledge of life at the best. He knows the business life of his business associates, but not their home life. He knows the home life of his friends, but not their business life. If he wants to know the whole life of a man, he has to pick up a book or go to the movies. But the country dweller sits in a movie every day of his life. All around him dozens of dramas are unfolding, episode by episode, with their rejoicings and their mournings; their births, marriages, and divorces; their triumphs and their despair. And the only admission price he pays is the reciprocal presentation of his own life drama, until such time as death removes him from the scene.

When the country dweller moves to the city, an interesting metamorphosis takes place. He cultivates, and very soon comes to feel, a blasé indifference to the private life of anyone but a movie actor, a multimillionaire, or a murderer. But in common with the rest of his fellow citizens, he goes after the most insignificant detail of the lives of these privileged classes like a starving cat after a bowl of cream.

To return to the herder. It is one of the privileges of his profession, as noted above, that he has abundant leisure to read. For hours at a time the sheep need nothing more than the herder's presence. Even when they are restless, there will still be several hours during the day in which he can read. If worse comes to worst and the sheep occupy all his time, there still remain his solitary evenings to be accounted for, and in fall and winter these evenings are long enough to satisfy the most omnivorous bookworm. I have heard of one or two sheepmen that objected to their herders reading, but I have never known a sheepman who failed to slip a book into his own pocket if for any reason he took the sheep for a while.

Reading sometimes serves other purposes than that of a pastime. If the herder on an intensely cold day can get interested in a good story, it will serve to take his mind off his other troubles, such as how much colder his feet will have to get before they crack and break off, and whether the sun is really standing still, or whether that is merely an optical illusion.

In my own case I have found that a steady diet of one kind of reading produces mental indigestion as quickly as a diet of one food would produce a like bodily effect. So I usually read the heavy stuff, political prognostications and such, in the morning, accompany my lunch with a story, and devote the afternoon to light and frivolous reading. I rarely take books out on the prairie, reserving them for evening reading, when they share the time with letter writing.

It would surprise the average person to know
the kind of periodicals that find their way into
sheep wagons. Country people are notoriously
more periodical-minded than city people, who
have their daily papers. You might come across
any one of the leading Eastern periodicals in the
sheep wagons of the plains, and you would find
that they were not only read, but digested.
The books might not average so high, being such
as the herder was able to borrow from his own or
neighboring ranches. There would be a liberal
sprinkling of Western stories among them.

But sometimes a herder gets into deep water.
I once tackled the poems of a woman mystic and
could n't make head nor tail of them. By way
of clarifying the situation and stimulating
thought, I absorbed a couple of stiff jolts of
hooch, waited for them to take hold, and tried
it again ; but with no better result. Suddenly I
realized that the fault lay not with the poetess,
but with myself. For if the average man does
not fully understand the average woman when
she is trying to express herself, what earthly
chance does he have when she is deliberately
trying to be mysterious ? He is simply fooling
away his time.

If quantity be the criterion, the herder ought
to be the best-read man in his community.

Certainly he has the most time for it, and doubt-less puts in the most time at it. "Reading maketh a full man," said one of the wisest men who ever lived. It is painful to think of the injustice that has been done to herders in the past by sheriffs and other peace officers who may have known their onions, but who apparently did not know their Bacon.

An aunt of mine once said that she did n't see why herders, with all the time they had at their disposal, did n't take up some line of study, like Chinese or astronomy. Now I never remember hearing of any herders who were addicted to these particular studies, but nevertheless they do take up certain lines of research and pursue them assiduously.

For instance, some herders take up the study of history, especially local history, and particu-larly personal private history, the kind that never gets into the history books — or into any other books. Some take up the study of statis-tics, and get so that they can predict probable increases in population — that is, among people they know. Of course they could n't be ex-pected to predict increases among people they did n't know.

Other herders take up the study of chemistry,

and try to find out what happens when you put some raisins and sugar and a little yeast in a jar of water and let them stand for a while. The only trouble with this experiment is that the herders are not patient enough to see the thing through to a finish. By the time that all the reactions should have been completed, the jar has been dry for some time, and so has the herder.

Many a herder takes up the study of psychology as revealed through facial expression, and tries to decide whether the poorly concealed delight on the face opposite him really denotes an ace full or merely a bob-tailed flush buoyed up by hope. This study has the advantage of adding to the herder's income, if he guesses right. The fact that it more often subtracts from that income than adds to it does not serve as a permanent deterrent. "Hope springs eternal . . ." as the poet remarked. The poet was probably lucky.

Finally, there are many herders who take up the study of physics, and try to find out what makes the jug remark, "Ug-ug-ug" when it is tipped up. It is incredible with what patient persistence they seek the answer to this question, performing the simple experiment over and over again until fatigue, or something else, causes them to postpone further experimentation till another time. There is something inspiring in the thought of this little band of scientists, patiently experimenting day after day, seeking no other reward other than that which they find in the work itself, furnishing their own materials, seeking no publicity — rather the contrary, if anything. What an example of unobtrusive devotion they set for scientists of the blatant, self-advertising kind !

It might seem that there is a hint of conscious illegality about this, but it is really not so. For if, as is commonly reported, the mountaineers of West Virginia are still voting for Lincoln, it is not surprising that there are a few herders out on the Great American Desert who have not yet heard of the passage of the Eighteenth Amendment.

In view of all the foregoing, it must be confessed that the herder does not have a New England conscience. This New England conscience is a fearful and wonderful thing. It is never happy unless it is driving its possessor to do something that makes him acutely unhappy or else is depriving him of the means for attaining happiness. So it comes about that a New Englander and his conscience can never be happy at the same time. If the New Englander is happy, it is a safe bet that his conscience is not.

Once upon a time New Englanders all had happy consciences, and their own joy in life may be judged from their portraits that have come down to us, portraits whose expression could probably not be matched to-day outside of a pickle factory. The herder manages a little better. He has his conscience under strict control. The herder leads, and his admiring conscience follows, and automatically registers approval of everything that he does.

While he is out on the prairie with his sheep, reading of course is the herder's principal amusement. This is often varied by friendly chats with passing riders. I knew one man who used to recite poetry as he herded. Some herders sing, and this custom is in great favor with the sheepmen; for when it comes to a choice between missing a mutton dinner or listening to a herder sing, the coyote usually discovers that he is not as hungry as he thought he was.

In the days before the Anti-Saloon League took over the congenial task of regulating the private lives of all nonmembers, when the herder went to town on his vacation his first stop would naturally be made at the saloon. If it was winter time, he needed something to warm him up; if it was summer, he needed something to cool him off; and if it was spring or fall, he needed to be fortified against sudden changes in the weather. On entering the saloon he would be sure to see some townsman he knew, probably one of the courthouse crowd, and would invite him to have a drink. After a short but fruitless pause to allow the townsman to reciprocate, the herder would set 'em up again. Thereafter he would not delay the game by waiting for the other to treat. Then, when he had tucked two or three more drinks under his belt, the herder would sally forth to attend to his less important business, his whole being aglow with kindly feelings toward the world in general and sociable townsmen in particular.

What the herder in the largeness of his heart failed to realize was that, while the country has always been the city's meal ticket, in the pre-Volstead era the countryside was the small town's bar bill as well. If any of the townsmen ever bought a drink, the editor of the local paper got out an extra describing the event, and there were low rumblings from the town lunacy board. In the language of the etiquette books of that day, it simply was n't done.

In those days when a sheepman came to town looking for a new herder, he would naturally apply to the saloon keeper. The latter would point out to him some herder who was flat broke.

There were two reasons for this. In the first place, if the herder had any money left, the saloon keeper would be loth to lose an actual as well as a potential customer; and in the second place, the herder would be unwilling to go as long as he had means for carrying on his private irrigation scheme.

Of course since prohibition all this has changed. Nowadays the herder banks every dollar of his wages, except about 40 per cent which he uses in buying babies' shoes. It is not that he has any children or expects to have any, but he knows from reading prohibition literature that all the money that was formerly spent on liquor now goes to buy shoes for the baby, and he feels that he must do his share. Now you tell one.

A herder sometimes sees strange sights while on vacation. Last summer while I was on a short trip, I saw a group of bankers giving away money. I need hardly add that they were intoxicated. There was a state bankers' convention in the town where I was changing trains, and a group of the bankers were pursuing a Salvation Army lass up and down the station platform and throwing money into her tambourine. You could tell they were bankers by the delegates' badges that they wore. But when I watched more closely and saw that each banker was throwing in ten cents and no more, I came to the conclusion that they were not so far under the influence as I had feared, and that the finances of our beloved country were still in safe hands. But probably the finances were safe in any case, for if those bankers had absorbed enough of the forbidden juice to induce them to contribute a quarter each, they would have been laid out in rows like cordwood.

Sometimes a herder's experiences on vacation are very sad. I had been attending a three-day convention in a South Dakota city, and on the last day of the convention there was a free dance in the evening. Being partly Scotch, I attended. I had been taking my breakfasts at the same restaurant every morning because the waitress was very pretty and the service was very good, and on account of this good service I had tipped her fifteen cents every time. Now at this democratic free dance I saw the beautiful waitress on the floor, and I thought to myself, "This is too easy!" and I approached and asked her for a dance. But this hash-slinger was either chuck-full of ingratitude or else fifteen cents meant nothing in her young life, because she politely but firmly declined the honor. I staggered across the hall and accosted the wife of one of the state officials, and she danced with me although she knew I was a herder, which the hash-slinger did not. If anyone should ask me why I asked the beautiful hasher before I did the state official's wife, I should have to answer that that is a secret known only to the entire male sex.

One of the most frequent and thoroughly enjoyable of the herder's simple pleasures comes when some neighboring herder drops in to spend the evening, when cards are forgotten, and sociability reigns supreme. Usually there will be a little preliminary cussing of the respective bosses for their latest high crimes and misdemeanors, this being more a matter of form than anything else, and a means of reasserting the great American principle of democracy. Then the talk will inevitably swing to the never-failing topic of the neighbors.

Some name will come up, and the class in vivisection takes the floor. The man is discussed dispassionately and completely. The herders will of course magnify his vices, explain away his virtues, gaze on the poor remains a few moments with gentle melancholy, and then pass to the next victim. Naturally the particular friends of each man, well known of course to the other, will be given unqualified praise ; or, if circumstances render this impossible, they will be passed over in a discreet silence.

Now it may be thought that in acting thus the two herders are guilty of unwarranted intrusion into a domain particularly reserved for the ladies. But the truth is that this being a frontier country, there is a real shortage of women, and consequently a certain proportion of their work, of the cooking, the dishwashing, and the gossiping, must be done by the men or not at all.

The countryside has a memory like a vise. It often forgives, but it never forgets. Consequently, because it took place in the country, we know that at the funeral of Methuselah, while the old fellows were tying their ox teams out behind the synagogue, they were recalling tales they had heard of the deceased's escapades in his teens and early twenties, nine hundred years previously; and in other groups their wives, such as were not engaged in consoling the widow, were probably doing the same.

Country people not only know all about each other, but they know the most intimate and hair-raising details about one another. Halitosis is nothing compared with the things they know, but don't mention to the person concerned. Many a man has believed that his family skeleton was safely locked in its closet, while in reality it was spending most of its time gallivanting around the country in a most unskeletonly manner. He should have known this was so, because he has at various times entertained the skeletons of all his neighbors. But by a merciful dispensation of providence, each one of us thinks of himself as an exception to any general rule.

If there is one thing that the city man prides himself on more than another, it is his sophistication; and this is the one thing that he is sure the country dweller lacks. Let us examine the case. Suppose that through some angelic dereliction of duty the Doomsday Book is left for a time unguarded, and that a city man and a countryman gain access to it. The city man sidles up to the book, and with the help of the index gets for the first time the real lowdown on his friends. With a tingling spine and a rising scalp lock he devours page after page. He finds that among his friends and acquaintances, men whom he thought he knew, one or another has been guilty of every crime in the calendar except chicken stealing, and a few moments' intensive thought convinces him that only the inconvenient location of the hencoops accounts for this omission. He closes the book with a shaking hand, and a no less shaken faith in human nature.

The countryman in turn approaches the book, opens to the section devoted to the misdoings of Windy Flat, and begins to read up on his neighbors. He reads a page and a half with growing boredom, and then closes the book with a gentle yawn. Old stuff; and incomplete at that.

XII

HAZARDS

At first sight it might seem that the herder, consorting with a notably harmless animal, living for the most part aloof from his fellow man, with no temptations other than those afforded by the mail-order catalogues, ought to lead a life singularly free from hazards of all sorts. But my belief is and my experience has been that the herder runs all the risks that other people do, with a few peculiar to his own profession thrown in for good measure.

I was undecided at first whether to include vacations under the heading of amusements or of hazards. Certain it is that vacation time has its share of dangers. When the herder betakes

himself from the peaceful serenity of flock tending to the bustle and hurry of modern life, it
takes a little while for him to adjust himself.
And when he leaves the society of the ewes all
modestly clad in wool from their ankles to their
eyes and then fares forth into the world and sees
what he does see, the shock is terrible. I have
heard it said that some herders wear blinders for
the first few days of vacation, until their eyes
become accustomed to the unaccustomed sights.
I almost got run down myself watching someone
cross the street.

Sometimes the herder runs into danger through
no fault of his own. Two years ago while on
vacation I was walking down one of the back
streets of Rapid City. There were no sidewalks
on this street, so I was walking along in the weeds
at the edge of the roadway. As I was rounding
a curve, I heard a car coming behind me, but
paid no attention to it, as I was not in the road.
The next instant I was struck violently in the
side and hurled to the ground, with just enough
breath left in me to utter the few words that
seemed most appropriate to the occasion. The
car, a coupé of the Elizabethan persuasion,
stopped a rod or two further on, and a girl came
running back.

Now if this had happened in a romantic novel

instead of in Rapid City, that girl would undoubtedly have flopped down in the dust, would have pressed my head to her bosom, and bathed my face with her tears. What she actually did do was to stand there and tell me to get up. It was a good idea, and I had already had it myself, but I lacked the necessary breath to carry it out.

Still I must not be too hard on the girl, for if I had been a hero of romance I should somehow have struggled to my feet, have laid my hand on my heart and assured her that the damage that her car had done to my clothing and parts adjacent was as nothing compared with the havoc that her beauty had wrought in my heart. But I was not a hero of romance, and besides, her general appearance was not such as to warrant a compliment of that high calibre. I was only a sheep herder on vacation, and she was just a modern girl driving a car recklessly with loose brakes. So I merely assured her that, brief as our acquaintance had been, the impression she had made on me would last for some time. She replied cordially that she hoped she might run across me again, upon which I very hastily bade her good-bye and thought the incident was closed.

But that afternoon as I was checking out of the hotel, the girl came up to the desk on the

same errand. She recognized me and said,
"Hello!" just to show that there were no hard
feelings on her part; and I answered in kind.
As she went out to where her car was parked
in front of the hotel, I watched her through the
big windows and thought to myself, "Now I 'll
see what effect this morning's accident has had
on her driving." I did see. She jammed in
the clutch and disappeared down the street in
a cloud of dust and gasoline smoke. With a
heart full of unrighted wrongs I turned to the
hotel clerk and said, almost accusingly, "That
girl knocked me down this morning." The clerk
made no answer, and I added, "That 's the first
time I was ever knocked down by a car."
"Oh!" said the clerk, a great light penetrating
his mental morasses, "it was the car that knocked
you down!" Some people are naturally low-
minded.

But being hit by a car is not the only risk we
run with this dangerous contrivance. This last
vacation I bought one. It was a case of love at
first sight, complicated with autohypnosis. The
car was a long blue monster, rakishly built, its
total length exceeded only by the length of the
list of things that ailed it. Even an inexperi-
enced eye could see that its fender was torn, that
its radiator was dented and leaking, and that one

lamp, gazing skyward, gave it the look of a cock-eyed bartender. But only a more experienced autoist would have noticed that its hind wheels did n't track; that it had two broken springs and three weak tires; that its battery gave few signs of life, its horn still fewer, and its speedometer none at all. Apart from these defects, however, nobody could deny that it was a good car. Shortly after I got it, a friend and I took a long trip with it. Of that trip, the less said the better. We had thirteen blow-outs in three days. Everyone expects the number thirteen to be unlucky, but when every number from one to thirteen is unlucky too, the going is tough. But, "Every cloud has a silver lining," as Pollyanna remarked. I took three inches off my waistline exercising with the tire pump, and my friend got rid of so much bad language while changing tires that by the time he got home he was practically pure. That night he was dreaming that he was still fixing tires, and he leaned over the edge of the bed and got a death grip on his trousers. If his brother had n't come in and waked him just in time, he would inevitably have put a tire patch on them.

The fact that a herder is alone in his wagon for a great part of the year involves certain dangers in case of sudden sickness. More than one herder has been found dead by the boss or camp tender. A friend of mine in social work in the East suggested that there ought to be a visiting nurse to make the rounds of the wagons and see that the herders were all right. This would probably meet with the unanimous approval of the herders, especially if they were allowed to pick out the nurse. But from the sheepmen's point of view it is terrible to think of the number of bands of sheep there would be wandering around on the prairie looking for their herders, while the herders were out looking for the nurse. Still, there is no doubt that the right kind of nurse, a big, fluffy-haired, blue-eyed blonde, for instance, could do wonders in prolonging the convalescence of almost any herder. In fact, he might easily slip into a state of chronic invalidism without even noting the change, or caring about it if he did.

Like all other mortals since the time man first cooked his meat instead of bolting it raw, the herder is subject to the hazards of fire. One day last spring at the beginning of lambing, I cooked breakfast for the other lamber and myself over a wood fire. I remarked to him that I would not use any coal, because we should not be in again till noon. We left the wagon about seven o'clock, and after I was outside I stepped back in again to make sure that I had closed the front draft. The wind was blowing a gale. Two hours later I saw the other lamber going toward the wagon with his horse on the run, but I thought that he was merely going back after some tobacco. I was talking at the time with one of the neighbors and had my back to the wagon, when all of a sudden he straightened in the saddle and shouted, "Look! Look!" I turned around and saw the wagon one mass of flames. I was a mile from where it stood, and afoot, so I could play only the part of a spectator, but the language in which I mourned the loss of my books, my clothing, and my typewriter started a prairie fire where I was standing.

The lamber first tried to get his tarp bed out from under the table, but it was firmly wedged there with his two suitcases behind it. Not knowing what else to do and not wishing to remain idle, he threw out in rapid succession the ink bottle, the salt cellar, and the sugar bowl. Just then his hair and his moustache caught fire, and he decided to leave. It is barely possible that he left before he fully decided. The man I had been talking to had in the meantime raced his horse to the wagon, and by a mixture of brain and muscle he succeeded in tipping off the burn-

ing upper portion, and thereby saved the running
gears. We found that the bottom of the stove
had rusted through just beneath the stovepipe.
A spark must have dropped through on to the
wood piled beneath, and there it smouldered for
two hours before bursting into flame.

But the greatest danger that the herder has
to face, in my opinion, is lightning. He is pecul-
iarly exposed to it. On the treeless plains of the
West, a man or a "critter" forms a natural target for the lightning bolt. Numbers of cattle
and still greater numbers of horses are killed in
this way every year. Most human beings naturally seek shelter at the approach of a storm,
but the herder must remain somewhere in the
vicinity of his sheep. They say lightning never
strikes twice in the same place. However that
may be, it is a safe bet that it never strikes the
same herder twice, if it gets a fair shot at him
the first time.

I knew a herder who was knocked unconscious
for several minutes when lightning struck a
bunch of sheep that he was driving into a corral.
Several of the sheep were killed and, strange to
say, the others started to pile up on top of them.
Another time a herder, who was taking my place
while I was on vacation, had gravel thrown into
his coat collar as he sat on his horse, when light-

ning struck a pebbly stretch of river shore just behind him. He too was rendered unconscious for some moments, and when he came to he was grasping the saddle horn to keep from falling.

My own closest call with lightning came several years ago. The wagon was perched on top of the highest hill in the neighborhood. A storm came up during the night, and as it drew nearer I sat up in bed and watched the sheep through the window in the back of the wagon. When the rain struck them they broke up into little groups, but did not go far because it was midsummer and the rain was warm. The lightning kept getting nearer and nearer, till suddenly there was a bolt and an almost simultaneous crash apparently right on top of the wagon. The thought flashed through my mind, "I might as well die lying down as sitting up," so I lay back on the bed and waited for the end of a perfect day. To my infinite relief the next crash sounded farther off. At daylight, not thirty paces from the wagon, I found four sheep dead, grouped closely, and already bloated, as is characteristic of lightning victims. Why the bolt should have struck such a comparatively low target as a sheep and should have ignored the wagon and its stovepipe, close by and on higher ground, is a question that must be answered by someone more intimately acquainted with lightning than I am. But at that, I do not crave any closer acquaintance with it than I have already had.

Not all herders are so lucky, however. Many a one has met his death from Jove's thunderbolt. In our own community several years ago there was Andy Swanson. He had intended to quit herding and go to California as soon as shearing was over. The last time his boss saw him alive, Andy said, "Well, Louie, I'm singing my last tune, and pretty soon I'll be going around them for the last time." That afternoon a small summer shower passed over — a mere sprinkle of rain, a few lightning flashes, and it was gone. The next day Andy's horse came to the ranch with the saddle on, but nobody thought anything of it, as it is no uncommon thing for a herder's horse to get away from him. But that evening was the time set for Andy to bring the sheep in to the ranch for shearing, and when he did not show up his boss went out to see what was the matter. He found sheep scattered everywhere, but no herder. Thoroughly alarmed, he summoned his neighbors, and all that night they hunted with lanterns and shouted, thinking that he might have fallen off a bank and broken a leg. At ten o'clock the next morning on a high rocky ledge they found him.

Andy had passed into the keeping of the Good Shepherd, who, if He disregardeth not the sparrow's fall, had surely in His infinite mercy already enfolded the soul of this poor herder who lay face downward upon the earth.

Sometimes danger strikes even more unexpectedly than the lightning bolt. A few years ago I was sitting in the wagon one sultry Sunday afternoon in midsummer writing letters. It was about half-past three and the sheep were leaving water, but had not yet gone far enough to need attention. Going to the door of the wagon to make sure they were all right, I found myself staring directly at an immense, black, bowl-shaped cloud, from the bottom of which a black snaky trunk sought the earth, the tip of it licking the dust from a ridge not half a mile away. I had seen such a sight once before, from the safe distance of three miles, but if I had never seen one I could not have mistaken it for any but the deadly thing that it was.

The wagon, as always in summer, stood on top of a hill. It occurred to me that a hilltop was about the poorest place imaginable in which to entertain a visit from a tornado. To be more accurate, I should say that this occurred to me as I was actively engaged in leaving. I know that I broke several records getting down that hill,

but since there was no one there with a stop
watch I don't know just which ones they were.
I reached the bottom and took out across the
flat with every intention of running out of the
path of that advancing column. But as I kept
track of it over my shoulder, it seemed to me
that I was running directly into that path. So I
turned and started back. Then I happened to
remember that there was an old homestead well
at the foot of the hill on which the wagon stood,
one of those shallow wells into which the homesteader would pour a barrel of water on the day
he proved up and then go to town and swear
himself black in the face that he had a well with
water in it. Into this five-foot well I let myself,
and from this favored spot watched the rest of
the proceedings.

I had been subconsciously aware all this time
of a great roaring in the air, but had put it down
to thunder. Now I noticed that it was unvarying and continuous, like the roar of great express
trains going by on either side. I saw the column
still advancing, and was amazed at its comparatively slow progress, since I knew that within
that whirling pillar the air was traveling at im-
measurable velocity. As I watched the advancing column, I saw it break in two, one part dropping toward the earth, the other withdrawing

toward the overhanging cloud; then the parts
joined again; then the lower end drew up and
let down quickly several times, as if it were rub-
ber bouncing on the earth. Higher and higher
were the bounces, and shorter became the trunk,
until finally it dissolved altogether into the gray
cloud above it, and its all-pervading roar became
merged into the new roar of an advancing hail-
storm.

Late that afternoon when the boss and his
family came out to see how everything was, I
learned that the tornado had struck a house
about four miles from where the wagon stood.
In the house at the time were a young mother
and four little girls. By the merest chance the
mother happened to glance out of the window
as the advancing column invaded the yard. She
had just time to throw the children on the bed
and fling a thick quilt over them, when the tornado struck. The walls seemed to press in and
then fell outward, the roof disappeared, and in
an instant the mother found herself flying
through the air. As she was carried along the
wind sucked her baby out of her arms, carried
it aloft, and then restored it to her; a board kept
gently tapping the back of her head; all she could
think of was broken bones, broken bones; then
quite suddenly she was on the ground with her

children around her, with broken and twisted farm machinery scattered all about them; and, on the very verge of collapse, she sent the eldest girl after one of the little ones, who, stripped of every shred of clothing, chased the flying column down the field, sobbing as she ran.

This storm performed the usual fantastic feats of its kind. Of the house it made matchwood. It flattened the barn, and piled the haystack upon it. It took hold of the steel tower of the windmill, twisted it as you would a piece of paper, and threw it to the ground. It stripped the chickens of their feathers and scattered their bodies everywhere. Of the comfortable farm home which it found, it left a desolate ruin.

This thing of being a nature lover is all right, and I yield to no one in admiration for Nature in all her moods. But when the clouds get so friendly that they drop down around the wagon and start wagging their tails, some other nature lover can have my place.

XIII

SHEEP HERDER AND COWBOY

ONE really ought to remove the hat in the presence of the cowboy, for undoubtedly he is dead. Every once in a while some noted author, living in the East, tries to apply a literary pulmotor to him. But the poor cowboy is beyond the aid of a pulmotor. Nothing short of a major miracle could be of any benefit to him. Confidentially and between friends, what the cowboy really needs is the friendly offices of an undertaker. So we should be free to honor his memory without the embarrassment of entertaining his unburied corpse.

For there are still men walking around in raiment which they claim is an authentic reproduction of "What the Well-Dressed Cowboy Will Wear," although the oldest living cowboys deny knowledge of any such costume. There is a real distinction between the old-time cow hands and the modern chap wearers. One of the former, who was attending a rodeo, said, "I looked around and saw what was wearing big hats, and then went and bought myself a cap." The old-time cowboys are now much more interested in how many miles they can get out of a gallon than in how many jumps they can get out of a bronc. I think we must admit that the fellow who rides around in chaps all day and then in the evening drives his car into town to the pool hall is not a cowboy in the generally accepted sense of the term.

It is amusing to watch the evolution of the modern cowboy. We see a boy going to school year after year, dressed like the rest of us in work shirt and overalls ; and then one day he blossoms out in full cowboy regalia, no detail missing, and another cowboy is born. Clothes may not make the man, but strip a cowboy of his big hat, his chaps, and his spurs, and it would take a whole detective agency to tell him from a hired man.

Granted without argument that it takes nerve, and lots of it, to mount a bronc that is likely to pitch. It takes still more nerve to be an aviator or a structural-ironworker. But, unlike the cowboy, the aviator and the ironworker do not on this account arrogate to themselves all the other virtues, together with a few of the more attractive vices.

Is there any intrinsic reason why the man who takes care of cattle should be a romantic, half-mythical figure, while the man who takes care of sheep is either a joke or anathema? Let us consider the two occupations a moment. The herder is in sole charge of fifteen to twenty thousand dollars' worth of property, and the safety and well-being of the sheep are largely dependent on his faithfulness and good judgment. The cowboy is not in actual charge of anything, but handles the stock from day to day as he is directed. The herder is his own boss a large part of the time, and plans his own work. The cowboy may be able to carry more than one day's orders in his head, but he seldom has the opportunity of proving it. The herder's wages run from ten to twenty dollars a month higher than the cowboy's in summer and are almost double the latter's in winter. But in spite of this, there is no denying the fact that every kid in the range country looks forward to the day when he can get hold of a pair of hair pants, a ten-gallon hat, a Miles City saddle, and a pair of big spurs, and then cultivate a bow-legged walk and hire out to a cattleman. If he ever has ambitions to grow up to be a herder, his family will never know it unless he talks in his sleep.

There is, perhaps, no truer illustration of the old copy-book aphorism which says that "men are only boys grown tall" than the celerity with which figures of national and even international importance, not any particular one, but numbers of them, no sooner touch the fringes of the cow country than they deck themselves out in full cowboy regalia, get in front of a camera, and look tough. Naturally the toggery does not make the celebrity a cowboy any more than a fringe of grass around his waist would make him a hula dancer, but a pleasing illusion to the contrary doubtless exists.

Speaking of toughness, years ago there was a certain saloon keeper in Bellefourche who had a Pintsch light out in front of his saloon at a time when such lights were a novelty, and consequently he was very proud of it. There was a certain young fellow in town who had been around the cows only a few days, and therefore was extremely tough and anxious to prove it. He wished to shoot out the lights in true cowboy fashion, but he believed he knew the ethics governing the situation. He entered the saloon

and, swaggering up to the bar, asked the proprietor, "How much will it cost me to shoot that
light out?" The old saloon keeper drew a
sawed-off shotgun from beneath the bar and
patted the stock affectionately. "Go right
ahead," he invited cordially. "It won't cost
you a cent!"

There is an almost universal belief that a cowboy's work is romantic. It may have been
once; but in the modern scheme of running cattle feed plays a very important part. In the
old days cattle had to depend on what they could
rustle themselves the year round. If the winter
was an open one, they came through in fine
shape. If it was a long winter with deep snow,
they died by thousands. But modern competition is too keen to tolerate a waste like that,
and nowadays the possibly once romantic cowboy gets very heavy on one end of a pitchfork.
He puts up hay for a couple of months during
the summer and he feeds it for many a long
month during the winter. In fact he puts in
from six to eight months a year handling hay in
one form or another, and then another month
or two handling the inevitable results. If this
be romance, make the most of it.

Those who still insist, however, that the cowboy's work is romantic may gesture in the direc-

tion of Hollywood and maintain that the cowboys there are simply reënacting their former
lives before the camera.   If they spent their real
cowboy days in rescuing satin-skinned heroines
and riding good horses to death, they probably
are ; but the chances are all against it.

The movie horse is a fearful and wonderful
animal.   Where the ordinary horse is content to
extract oats from a nose bag, the movie horse
prefers to extract the cube root of an unknown
number in the mind of his rider, and then polish
off the performance with a lecture on the fourth
dimension.   The movie horse cannot walk, he
cannot trot, he cannot even lope decently.   He
knows nothing but a senseless and headlong run.
And this pace, which would burst an ordinary
horse wide open in a mile or two, the movie
horse can keep up indefinitely, up hill and down.
With equal facility he charges up slopes that
would make a Rocky Mountain goat dizzy, and
he slides down precipices that an even ordinarily
cautious housefly would n't attempt without
chains.   The movie horse leaves Jersey City one
hour late, and he overtakes the west-bound limited just as it is slowing down to two miles an
hour to pass through Philadelphia.   The movie
horse has not yet beaten an airplane in a straightaway, but give him time, give him time.

In the range country, if you see a distant horsebacker traveling at a lope, it is an entirely safe bet that the rider is either a woman or a kid. A kid's business is always important and, besides, he does n't know any better, and women actually, as well as proverbially, have very little mercy on a horse. A man rider realizes that his horse, like himself, has just so much strength to give; and that if it is wasted when there is no need, it will not be there to draw upon when need comes. Therefore he proceeds no faster than a trot, a pace which is hard on him, but easiest for the horse.

Consider for a moment the two outstanding cowboys, the one of life, the other of literature, Will Rogers and the hero of *The Virginian*. The latter received his early training and the full impress of his character in Virginia. This fully formed character and his Southern accent he took to the West. His chaps and his guns were accidental and incidental. In his essence he was and remained simply a transplanted Virginian. In like manner Will Rogers is uniquely and inimitably Will Rogers, the darling of the gods and the delight of mankind, and millions have laughed at his wit who never had a chance to laugh at his chaps. Both of these men possessed remarkable personalities, and both would have been equally remarkable if they had never even seen a cow and had never learned how to hog-tie a steer or throw the bull.

When we consider the position of the sheep herder in literature, we find that he fares no better there than he does in life. He is apparently limited to two rôles. He either serves as an animated target for the drunken and high-spirited cowboy or, himself drunk, serves as a foil for the virtuous, noble, and high-minded cowboy. Once, in an O. Henry story, we find a herder who is apparently on the road to being the hero, but he turns out to be an escaped convict, still on the down grade.

The herder really yearns for higher things. He would like to follow the cowboy's example as the latter rides in concentric circles around the schoolhouse, looking for the locoed heifer that was last seen in that vicinity three years before. But, alas! the herder has a standing engagement with the sheep thirty-one days out of the month. He would like to rescue the schoolma'am from a fate worse than death, but the chances are that the schoolma'am would prefer even that fate to the ignominy of being rescued by a herder. But when the ignorant herder sees the cowboy risk his neck in breaking a bronc for five dollars, he comes to the conclusion that either the cowboy's neck is worth only five dollars or that his brains are located in that portion of his anatomy which clings most closely to the saddle. It is the novelists, later aided and abetted by the scenario writers, who have elevated the cowboy to his present position somewhere between heaven and earth, who have crowned his noble brow with all the laurel and bays there are, and who have arranged all the spokes and felloes in his halo; and until the novelists experience a change of heart, or until someone punctures their hero's gas bag, the attitude of the herder toward his ancient rival must be as that of one looking up.

Throughout a large part of the West to-day, cowboy stuff is merely a phase which boys pass through, like playing Indians or soldiers, only some of them never grow up. There will probably always be in the West a certain type of young fellow who cannot go out and drive in the milk cows without buckling on chaps and spurs. But with the present stringent laws against murder, there is probably nothing that can be done about this. It is all a part of life in the great open spaces, where cowboys will be cowboys and where *The Virginian* is still widely read — as a book of etiquette.

The good old days when the cowman and his cowboys used to tie the herder to the wheels of his wagon and club his sheep to death by the hundreds or drive them over a cutbank — those days are gone forever. To-day each rancher, whether sheepman or cattleman, uses and pays for his own grass as a rule, and range quarrels are no longer carried on over a wide front "from the Alps to the sea," but are local and individual affairs.

Every cattleman knows that sheep ruin the range for cattle, and that cattle dislike to graze where sheep have been — refuse to, in fact. Every cowman knows this and makes no secret of it, but proclaims it in season and out. The only trouble is that the cowmen have n't taken their herds into their confidence, and the result is that the cattle, never having been informed of their inhibitions, graze wherever they think the grazing is good, and they show a particular fondness for the grass that grows rich and rank on old sheep bed grounds. According to information in the hands of the cattlemen, they ought to shun spots like this as a beauty-contest winner would a smallpox sign.

No one wishes that this theory of the cattlemen were true any more fervently than does the sheepman. If it were true, he would be saved many a long ride chasing stray stock off his range, and his grass would go to market entirely surrounded by wool, instead of going to swell the commissariat of his neighbors' wandering herds.

"It cost me five hundred dollars to be a neighbor to that man," remarked a cattleman of his neighbor, a sheepman. What he really meant was that the sheepman had insisted that he keep track of his cattle, just as the sheepman kept track of his own stock. In other words, the sheepman pays one thousand dollars a year, the amount of his herder's board and wages, for the privilege of knowing where his stock is at all times. It is not unreasonable for him to insist that the cattleman make some effort to acquire a similar knowledge with regard to his own stock. The only apparent solution is a line fence. But since the sheepman still has to employ a herder as before, and since the cattleman's fence is in effect a herder hired once for all and paid in full, it is evident that the cattleman still has far the better of it as far as expense goes. And in this he is lucky, for his income is decidedly less than that of the sheepman in proportion to invested capital.

It would be an interesting psychological problem to determine why the average farmer or cattleman can view with apparent equanimity the presence of strange cattle or horses on his range, and yet at the sight of sheep on the same range be reduced to a state bordering on apoplexy, complicated further by homicidal tendencies. There somehow seems to be a strong, deep, and unreasoning prejudice against sheep on the part of practically everyone who does not own them. There seems to be no middle ground with regard to them. You are either for or against, whole-heartedly and completely.

Upon retiring at night the pious sheepman puts up a petition that his herder knows where all his sheep are — safe on the bed ground. About the same time the cattleman is praying fervently that nobody but himself knows where his cattle are — on his neighbors' grass. Ordinarily the cattleman when confronted with the evidence falls back on his one cast-iron alibi: "I did n't know they were there; I 'll send over and get them." Usually this is considered good for three hundred and sixty-five days in the year, but in leap year it will be used three hundred and sixty-six times. When the herder is caught across the line with his whole bunch, about the only really effective alibi he has is to utter a plaintive blat, drop on his knees, and start cropping grass.

Both cattle and sheep are subject to wide fluctuations in price. For the past several years and up to a recent date, cattle have been in a prolonged slump. In many places it has been the sheepman's money that has kept the banks going. As one sheepman rather undiplomatically remarked, "We sheepmen have been tailing you cattlemen up for the last three years." It is the truth that hurts, they say, and when the cattleman realizes the strong economic position of his despised rival, and especially the latter's better standing at the bank, then the cattleman experiences a sharp and shooting pain between the small of his back and the cantle of his saddle.

A sheriff in a Western town, zealous for prohibition enforcement, arrested a sheepman who had a suspicious bulge on his hip. It turned out that the bulge was the money the sheepman had left over after paying his bills. The sheriff apologized publicly for having arrested him, but at the same time he announced that any cattleman displaying a similar bulge would be forthwith thrown into the calaboose without even being searched.

There is somewhere in the West a cattleman whose wife some years ago went into sheep on her own account and with her own money. For the last three years it has been her sheep money

that has bought feed for her husband's cattle.
The strangest part of this true story is that the
couple in question are still living a happy married life.   If matrimony as an institution can
come unscathed through a test like that, surely
it is destined to endure forever.

Sheep are somewhat more expensive to run
than cattle, but they produce two money crops
a year, the lambs and the wool.   These two crops
are marketed several months apart, the wool in
the spring and the lambs in the fall.   So the
sheepman has ready money twice a year, whereas
the cattleman has but one harvest.   If the
cattleman could skin his entire bunch every
spring at a trifling cost and sell the hides for a
fourth of what the cattle themselves were worth ;
if the cattle would then walk about happily and
grow more hides for next year's skinning ;   if
he could sell his calves every fall for about two
thirds of what their mothers were worth — if
he could do all this in place of his present system
of marketing his stuff, then the cattleman could
hold up his head and take his place with the
sheepman.

XIV

HOMESTEADS

SCIENTISTS tell us that the strongest of human instincts is that of self-preservation, and that next to that comes preservation of the race; but somewhere well up among the headliners will be found that instinct which bids men strive to get something for nothing. This it is that sends men into the frozen wastes of the North for gold, to torrid Africa after diamonds, and to the ends of the earth after oil; this it is that sprinkles the pages of our advertising with that most alluring word FREE!! and with that stern warning, "Send No Money"; this it is that heaps the gentler sex in a writhing mob against the bargain counter with scant regard for courtesy and corns; and this it is that has sent men and women by the tens of thousands out into the unoccupied spaces, there to wager fourteen months of their time against a hundred and sixty acres of government land — and lose.

The general idea was that the Government would give a quarter section of land to anyone who would furnish proof of his intention to make it his permanent home. The conditions necessary to this proof were carefully set forth and consisted roughly of three years' residence, some cultivation, a water supply, and a habitable dwelling. There was a provision that if the homesteader wished to commute his residence to fourteen months' time, he might do so on the payment of a dollar and a quarter an acre at the time of proving up. The vast majority of homesteaders adopted this plan, because by the time fourteen months were past some doubts were usually beginning to intrude themselves as to the ultimate cost of this free land. They used to say that there was no cure for the land fever except filing — that is, taking up a homestead. But if the Keeley and associated cures had annihilated thirst as completely as homesteading did the land fever, we should probably never have needed a Volstead law.

The Government theoretically demanded proof that the homesteader intended to make the land his permanent home, and yet no one knew better than the Government that for the individual homesteader to remain on his bare hundred and sixty acres would be equivalent to suicide by the painful process of slow starvation. Knowing this, the Government accepted the proofs required, issued patent to the land, and, after satisfying itself that there had been no glaring fraud committed, washed its hands of the whole affair and crossed the land off its books. Since it is estimated that if one in ten of the original settlers of a country remain, it is a high average, it is apparent that homesteading is simply the process of getting the land out of government control and into private ownership.

In the interpretation of the Government's very lenient requirements, there was an extremely broad divergence among homesteaders, and the tendency to stretch conscience to its extreme limits and beyond. In fact, it might be said that the land laws were as carefully observed as the later Prohibition law has been. Of course there was some suspicion of this on the part of the officials who received the homesteaders' oaths, but as one of them remarked, "We are n't doing the swearing." Obviously if a man came in from forty miles out on the prairie and swore that he had lived on his claim the whole of the fourteen months, the United States commissioner was in no position to dispute him. The only trouble could come through some of the man's neighbors. The Scotch have a saying, "He sits full still that has a hole in his breeks," and where a neighborhood is fairly well sprinkled with breeks that need the attention of a tailor, there are not likely to be many who will risk parading around and calling attention to themselves.

Of course there were all degrees of observance, because there were all sorts and conditions of "honyocks," as the homesteaders were called. There was the man who wrote the Government asking if he might leave his claim after dark, providing he returned to it before daylight, and there was the man who never slept overnight on his homestead during the whole time he was supposed to be in residence. There was the man with a vivid imagination who, in answer to the question as to how many acres he had ploughed, answered, "Between eleven and twelve," because he had a distinct mental concept of a twelve-acre patch on one side and an eleven-acre patch on the other side of the one furrow he had drawn, probably a crooked one. This excursion into the realms of higher mathematics was more complicated than the expedient adopted by several unfortunate ones, who thoughtfully primed their dry wells with a barrel or two of water, so that they might go before the commissioner and swear with a clear conscience that they had a well with water in it. There was the man who confused what he had done with what he intended to do, and what eventually he never got around to doing. But to offset these there were vast numbers of men and women who stayed their time, lived up to the law, and received their reward — such as it was.

A homestead community is like nothing else on the face of this earth. A gold rush or an oil boom brings out a certain type of man, who behaves in a foreseen manner. It is practically a stag affair. A homestead community, on the other hand, is a mixture of sexes, ages, race, and condition. It would be hard to imagine a more heterogeneous group than the average homesteaded landscape would bear. There would be mechanics, farm laborers, kitchen mechanics, clerks, schoolma'ams, lawyers, nurses, preachers, ex-soldiers, merchants, and musicians — every class and occupation you could think of. The high-school teacher would be for a year or more

thrown into close neighborly relations with a
class of men that she would never have met in
her home town.   Who can doubt that all of them
profited by the association ?   As for nationalities,
in one dance crowd of about seventy-five people
we counted twenty-three distinct racial strains.

In homesteading, a whole countryside is apt
to settle up at one time, because when the
locators have found certain section corners it is
comparatively easy to find others in the same
region.   The locator would tie a handkerchief
around one of his buggy spokes, set his course
by compass, and so many revolutions of the
buggy wheel would bring him into close proximity with the next corner stone.   Therefore,
as soon as he got a new prospect for land, he
would take him to where he had located the last
one, and introduce him to his new neighbor.
The locator received anywhere from twenty-five
to one hundred dollars, whatever he thought the
traffic would bear, for showing the prospect a
piece of vacant land and finding the corners for
him.   But it was when a number of families
came from one community that the locator's
real harvest began.   These families, having
known each other in their former homes and
having made the trip out together, naturally
would wish to file close together, and as the

locator was eager to file them just that way, everyone was satisfied. However, these community removals were the exception rather than the rule, and the filings were usually singles or a group of two or three made by members of one family. Any man over the age of twenty-one and any unmarried woman or widow of that age was eligible to file.

Sometimes the mere fact of filing together would not satisfy the gregarious longings of those concerned, and they would erect their shacks within a few feet of each other, each on his own side of his line. But it must be regretfully recorded that in some instances the familiarity induced by such close proximity bred so much contempt that both shacks would eventually be yanked to the far end of their respective claims, and communication between them would cease.

At first there would be, in a homestead community, the most absolute democracy to be found anywhere. Everyone started on an equal footing. Everybody would perforce take everybody else at his own valuation, since there was no other standard to go by, and this self-valuation in some cases proved to be a trifle high. There would be community dinners on special occasions, community picnics, and community love feasts. But the serpent could not be forever absent from this Garden of Eden, and by and by some of the community's citizens would begin to acquire reputations, and others would have reputations furnished for them by their loving friends. Some member of a group that came from the same locality would casually inform one of his new neighbors that a certain woman of the group shed her reputation about the time she did her milk teeth, or that a certain man of the group once whipped the gold filling out of the tooth of a blind man who had too confidingly opened his mouth to ask him the way to the Y. M. C. A. The listener would casually file these items away as interesting but unrelated facts. Later, however, when he had traded everything but his trousers and suspenders to this man for something that he was ashamed to take home when he had the opportunity to examine it closely, or when his wife had caught the before-mentioned woman trying to vamp her favorite husband, then a coolness would arise between them such as would cause the whole community to put on their winter underwear a month ahead of time.

Once the seed of suspicion had been sown, the harvest of tares would grow rapidly, watered by the gossip of a community that had little to do, plenty to eat, and nothing whatever to worry

about. There was one particular community
containing several grass widows, and they say
that the mortality rate of reputations in that
region was something frightful, someone's reputation being sure to be murdered every time two
of the grass widows got together. But in any
homestead region, by the time the fourteen
months were up and the exodus had begun, there
would be a certain number of people who would
not be on speaking terms with others, and even
among the rest there would be certain doubts,
private opinions, and mental reservations.

While the exodus was never as sudden as the
influx, still it would be more rapid than would
be the case in any other kind of community.
The whole cycle of homesteading would last little
more than three years. First there would be the
raw prairie, in the same state in which the ages
had left it; then almost overnight there would
be a tar-papered shack, or a sod shanty, or a
dugout on every arable quarter section, with
people walking across the landscape at all hours
(an unheard-of thing in a range country), with
people going in groups to the post office and in
shoals to community picnics and dances. Then,
a year or two later, there would be open cellars
where the board shanties had stood, roofless sod
walls nodding into ruins, and fields growing up to

weeds and grass again. A few years more, and
the fields are well-nigh obliterated, the old neighborhood trails can barely be traced, and here and
there a low mound of earth, not yet grass-grown,
would be all that would mark the spot where
some adventurer had put up his sod shanty,
stayed his time, won his wager with the Government — and lost.

For if they win, they lose. Nine out of ten
of the heterogeneous mob that comes out to
take up homesteads could have made more in
the same length of time by sticking to their own
trade or profession. True, when they prove up
they have a hundred and sixty acres of land to
sell, and so has everyone else. And there are no
buyers. There are, or rather were, loan companies that would lend a certain amount against
the land. Very few indeed of these companies
are still in existence, because most of them went
to smash when they found themselves loaded
down with land on which the owners had grown
tired of paying interest and taxes.

And yet it may be doubted whether many of
the homesteaders regretted their lost time and
money. It was an experience such as they had
never had before and could never have again,
because the man who homesteads once is
through. It would always remain for them a

subject for reminiscent thought and a topic of conversation. For a large share of them it was the only time in their lives when they were actual land owners, and the ownership of land, even of land that nobody wants, brings with it a certain satisfaction. An aunt of mine, who visited me when I was still on my claim, summed it up in this way, "It is a nice thing to have done." The accent was on the *have*.

XV

THIS IS THE LIFE!

I HAVE often wondered why the editors of some woman's magazine have not written to one or another of us herders requesting light on housekeeping problems — some snappy article, for instance, like "Housekeeping in Its Simpler Forms; or, Why Wash the Dishes?" Perhaps these editors do not know the unrivaled opportunities that a herder has for studying these problems with an undivided mind. The average woman has so many different angles to her job that she cannot concentrate on the strictly housekeeping end of it. For instance, she has to worry about whether Buster's hair and the front

lawn need cutting; whether her husband is regarding her approvingly enough and whether he
is regarding anyone else at all; whether she shall
relax comfortably into a stylish stout, or whether,
following the dictates of fashion, she shall strive
to attain the general proportions and attractive-
ness of a bean pole, on the theory that by destroy-
ing the last visible vestiges of her womanhood
she will thereby strengthen her womanly lure —
a proposition which only feminine logic would
set for itself and which nothing short of black
magic could ever resolve.   The herder has none
of these worries.   The figure on his pay check
interests him intensely, but to the figure inside
his overalls he is vastly indifferent.   Consequently he is able to concentrate on the funda-
mental problem of getting three meals a day,
stowing them away, and cleaning up afterwards.

When I first began to "bach," I was as green
as it was possible to be.   I did not know that
bacon could burn, and I thought you had to boil
potatoes before you fried them.   One thing I
did not do, and that is, fill a kettle full of beans,
set it on the stove, and then fill successively
every utensil in the house with the inevitable
overflow.   I not only did not do this, but I
believe I am the only bachelor who has never
claimed that he did.   They say forewarned is

forearmed. My great-great-grandfather kicked the bottom out of his crib the first time he heard that story. Certainly I have heard it from the cradle up.

There really ought to be a way of disposing of these old jokes that have weathered the centuries and resisted the teeth of time. Probably one anthropoid ape in the dawn of the ages chattered them aimlessly into the ear of another ape, just before being struck violently with the nearest available rock or club. These jokes were not funny in the first rosy dawn of civilization and, like the cold-storage eggs of the same vintage, they have not improved with age. It would be useless to pension them, because they would continue to work on regardless. The only solution is to give them that sepulture which is so many thousand years overdue, and then if any ghoul in human form is caught prowling around trying to disinter them, he should be quietly but firmly buried beside them, without even a headstone to mark his dishonored grave.

To return to baching, my first three years of it were during the time I was homesteading. Another like-minded bachelor stayed with me for a while, and we lived as bachelors should n't, but often do. We swept the floor only when one of us had lost some money, and we made the bed,

if at all, just before we got into it at night.   My
companion was called the cook, but this was a
title of courtesy only, because he knew even less
about cooking than I did.   Whenever he could
not think of anything else to get for dessert, he
produced what he called "floating island."
That is, he concocted a pale, flabby mixture of
doubtful appearance and uncertain antecedents,
and in the centre of it he put a dab of jelly.
During his incumbency I ate enough floating
island to dry-dock the entire United States navy.

One day he produced his masterpiece, a pie.
The filling was of what we call buffalo berries,
and there were strips of dough crisscrossing it
like a gridiron.   We greatly admired it as a work
of art, but since we knew a good deal about its
composition we did not venture to tackle it ourselves.   However, we ceremoniously put it on
the table whenever we had company.   But
somehow the company seemed to have certain
suspicions of their own, and while they evinced
a lively curiosity in the pie as a museum piece,
they unanimously and consistently declined to
sink their teeth into it.   In time the pie came
to have a somewhat tired and shopworn appearance, which was not surprising in view of the
mileage to its credit from the cupboard to the
table and return ; the strips of dough seemed to

rest more heavily on the filling beneath; and the buffalo berries lost their rosy blush and acquired a sombre and melancholy hue (it being impossible to dust them). Finally, its last appearance, we set the pie before a friend of ours who had dropped in to dinner. He regarded it a long time with a fascinated gaze. We urged him to have a piece of it. "No, thank you," he said politely, "I don't think I care for any. But I would like to know what kind of a flytrap you used."

This alleged cook did not know at first that there was any difference between cooking soda and washing soda; to his literal mind soda was soda. Consequently the first batch of biscuits that he made, sixteen years ago, are still decorating the hillside below the shack, unless someone in the meantime has hauled them away for building material. If they had been the right size and shape they would have made excellent tombstones, and if we had eaten them that is what we should have needed. It was common report in the neighborhood that the cook used his biscuits to cripple the neighboring jack rabbits so that his dog could catch them.

After a while another man joined us. He was scrupulously clean and a good cook, and the memory of his macaroni and cheese lingers with me to this day. For a short while the three of us lived together, and since our first names all began with the letter *A*, we called the place the Crazy A Ranch. There was an innocent-appearing jackass roaming the prairies in that neighborhood, and on the strength of his initial we elected him to honorary membership. One of the brethren was returning to the shack late one pitch-black night, and, unknown to him, the honorary member was standing right beside the trail. Perhaps the newly elected one had heard of the honor and wished to voice his thanks. At any rate, when the returning brother was just opposite him, the jackass delivered fraternal greetings against his eardrums from a distance of about four feet. Now a jackass has a voice like an ungreased buzz saw with a bad cold roaming through a pine knot regardless, and the effect of this, crashing suddenly through the black stillness of a prairie night, may be better imagined than described. Suffice to say that the returning brother immediately executed a standing jump of remarkable height, and only his heavy cap prevented his hair from pointing heavenward.

When I began to herd, I found that I had to make some changes in my way of baching. Meals had to be eaten at stated hours and not as the spirit moved. They also had to be substantial ones. Furthermore, there was someone else who checked up on the housekeeping end, and lax methods were looked on with disfavor. But in the course of the years two things have impressed me with regard to housekeeping, and I am willing to impart them freely to anyone for what they are worth.

In the first place I found out that this idea of meal planning is, vulgarly speaking, the bunk. I did all my meal planning ten years ago, and since then have had my mind free for more important things, as, for instance, how to meet that overdraft at the bank. The plan is simplicity itself: I have the same things for the same meals every day. It might seem that this diet would grow monotonous, but my single boarder has never complained; in fact, he has thrived on the simple fare, and in the course of years his belt buckle has gradually been pushed farther from his backbone. The proof of the pudding is in the eating, and I am the living proof of the correctness of my theory.

The second point that strikes a herder is the unnecessary amount of time that a woman devotes to housework. A herder has finished his housework for the day fifteen minutes after breakfast is over. By that time he has washed the dishes, swept the wagon, and brought in the wood and coal for the next twenty-four hours. I really cook only one meal a day, at noon or at night according to the season. For this meal I fry a skillet level full of potatoes, eat half then, and save the other half for the backbone of another meal. When thoroughly reheated until they sizzle, the potatoes are as good as if they were fresh fried. The third meal, if there is one, is a pick-up. But for six months out of the year the third meal is a lunch eaten out on the prairie. Taking into account cooking, cleaning up, and all else, the herder does not spend more than an hour and a half a day in housework.

But although I feel that I have learned a point or two of value as to cooking and housework, this assurance does not extend to the washing of clothes. My first experience with that was disastrous. I put the clothes all together first into boiling water and then into cold. But whereas they had a certain individuality when they went into the water, they had an alarming similarity when they emerged from it. The only thing that looked natural was a dark gray suit of underwear. It was still dark gray. But so was my handkerchief. It might easily have done duty as a mourning band or a Jolly Roger, but as an article of adornment and a badge of decency it was a washout.

As one star differeth from another in glory, so there are many grades and degrees of housekeeping ability among bachelors. There are some who can and do keep as clean a house and cook as good meals as any woman, and in addition to that do a good day's work outside. Fairness, however, compels the admission that few of them have a houseful of children to care for besides. There are also bachelors of the opposite kind. But as the extreme modesty of those concerned prevents the good examples from being singled out, so self-preservation forbids any identifying allusion to the latter.

It is inevitable that in a frontier country where there is a surplus of bachelors, the subject of matrimony should come up for frequent discussion. Back in the days when this part of the country was being homesteaded, there were three men on a trip to some distant hills after firewood. They stopped for the night at the house of an old-timer, and shortly after supper two of them spread their bed on the kitchen floor and turned in. The other man sat at the table keeping company jointly with his host and a jug which the wood haulers had brought along in case of snake bite, a common precaution in those days. The host, who did not drink, was carrying a heavy load of worry and apprehension. He had become engaged some time before to a heart and hand woman, and she was soon to come out and join him, and he was suffering from a touch of prenuptial cold feet, such as seems to be the lot of the average male. He said that he did not have much to offer a woman, but that he hoped he might make her happy. He was a sober, earnest-minded fellow, and as he spoke of the seriousness of the step he was taking, the tears came to his eyes. The sight of these tears was too much for the man with the jug, who by this time had developed a crying jag, and he broke down completely. In a voice choked with sobs he informed his host that the latter's sentiments were among the very noblest that had ever come to his attention. So these two men sat there by the kitchen table with tears streaming down their faces, discoursing in broken voices of the dangers and pitfalls of matrimony, while the two men on the floor were shaking the house with their suppressed laughter.

It can hardly be denied even by the married, or perhaps especially by the married, that bachelorhood has certain advantages of its own. It is worth something to be able to form your own opinions about people and things, instead of having to use a lot of secondhand ones that don't fit; to be able to take a drink if you want it, or let it alone if you can't get it; to be able to appropriate to your own use and behoof the entire contents of the pay envelope, or such part of it as the bank does not already have covered by two mortgages and a prior lien; and best of all, at the end of the day's work to be able to look forward to an uninterrupted evening of doing the things you want to do, not the things someone else wants to do, nor the things someone else thinks you ought to want to do.

Still, he is a very stubborn and pig-headed man who is not open to conviction, and if any of you know of a young girl contemplating matrimony (perhaps you don't know any other kind), preferably the winner of a beauty contest within a year or two; one who has an independent income which in case of necessity could and would be stretched to cover the needs of two; who would enjoy living in a small, portable habitation, where she would have a complete change of scenery every six weeks, where there is no upstairs work, and where she could do up the housework in fifteen minutes after breakfast and have the rest of the day to read, sleep, or do window shopping in Montgomery Ward and Sears, Roebuck; a girl who would like to spend her evenings doing fancywork in silence unless her husband preferred to talk; who would not mind taking the sheep out on particularly cold and stormy days (just for the novelty of the thing, you know); who would regard her husband with intense and single-minded devotion, but who would not be too critical if his eyes and affections should chance to wander a trifle (we're all human, of course) — if you know of a girl like that, don't even wait to telegraph; just send her out. It will be all right with me.

When the old Quaker remarked to his wife, "All the world is queer but me and thee; and thee's a little queer," he unconsciously furnished an alibi for the herder and other solitary workers. From the standpoint of the average city man or even the ranch hand, it might seem queer that a man would deliberately choose to consort with sheep rather than with his fellow men, choose to live a more or less solitary life, to do his own cooking, and to work Sundays, holidays, and the Fourth of July. But, on the other side of the fence, the herder never ceases to wonder why the ranch hand will put in almost the same hours and work infinitely harder, when he might make much higher wages sitting on a hillside and watching a bunch of sheep.

Of course there are certain temperaments that would never find life in a sheep wagon endurable. A man who feels the need of constant companionship would never dream of herding. Neither would a man who had no resources within himself, but must constantly look abroad for entertainment. Also there are some, as hinted previously, who look down on sheep, on herding, and on herders, and they are not confined to the chap-wearing portion of the community. Finally there are some who, to put it charitably, feel the need of exercising their backs, because they have very little to exercise just beneath the part in their hair.

But just as there are many who will not herd, so there are others who will not do anything else, as long as they can get a bunch of sheep to watch. They have tried the life, like it, and they stick to it. As to what started them on their downward career, there could probably be no general answer. I can only give my own experience, and I do not know whether it is typical or not.

When I began to herd, the boss said to me, "Herding is what you make it." In that brief statement he put the whole lure of herding. In other words, it leaves a man free to live his own life. It may seem strange at first sight to speak of freedom in connection with an occupation that ties the worker to his job seven days in the week and cuts him off more or less from his fellow man. But it so happens that the same conditions that enslave the herder's body are the very ones that free his mind. They prevent the herder's feet from taking him more than a mile or two in any one direction, but they leave his mind free to roam that other world which knows no bounds save those of time and space.

If a farm hand gives his boss an honest day's work, he is likely to be tired at night and fit only for bed. The same is doubtless true in numberless other lines of work. But such an ending to the day is an exception for the herder. Occasionally he may come back to the wagon in the evening so tired that he can scarcely drag one foot after the other, but this is distinctly the exception. Usually he will be as fresh at night as he was in the morning. He will have had an abundant opportunity to read during the day, and he can look forward to an uninterrupted evening of reading, writing, solitaire, or whatever he wishes.

Like most country dwellers I subscribe to a number of magazines, fifteen at the present time.

I also have a library of about five hundred volumes, to which I am constantly adding. So I am abundantly supplied with reading matter. For purely personal reasons I am deeply interested in a certain figure in English literature, Samuel Pepys. I have borrowed from the university library and have bought many a volume concerning him and his times, and I expect to buy and borrow many more. If for any reason my interest in him should wane, there are a hundred other bypaths that beckon. The heritage is inexhaustible; it is only a question of choice.

There was formerly a community dedicated to the principles of plain living and high thinking. Almost any herder might have applied for charter membership there. As to the plainness of his living there can be scarcely any argument. It is true that when the boss or the sheep misbehave, the thinking of the herder is apt to be decidedly low, not to say coarse. But no one can stand the rarefied atmosphere of Everest's peak, and those who attempt even its upper slopes must carry their oxygen with them. The herder has at least the privilege and opportunity of climbing as high as he is able.

The herder's life is a free one in still other ways. He is cut off from many of the benefits of civilization, but he is also free from many of its shackles. He can boast of freedom from the insistent telephone, from the mammoth and time-wasting daily papers, from the evening-destroying movies, and from the thousand and one petty distractions of city life that take a man's time and sap his strength without adding proportionately to his happiness, until he becomes the passive recipient of whatever impact the next moment may bring.

The West is proverbially freer than the East, its people a little more unconventional, a little more hospitable, a little more open-hearted. They are a little more apt to say what they mean and mean what they say. When a Westerner makes a remark, you do not have to go through a system of mental calisthenics to decide just what he means by it. The apparent meaning is likely to be the real one. All these traits are apt to be still further intensified in a frontier section of the West, and it is only in a frontier country that sheep can be run profitably in large bands. Land at two hundred and fifty dollars an acre may be all right for the raising of corn, but land at two dollars and fifty cents an acre is a better bet for the raising of sheep.

As to the great open spaces that you hear so much about, we have them, at least if by that you mean a great open space between neighbors.

During vacation a few years ago, while on a Lake boat I met a man from Buffalo, New York.   I said to him, "Every time you mention Buffalo, you make me homesick.   That is the name of my home town, Buffalo, South Dakota."   "How big is it?" he asked.   "A hundred and twenty-five."   "A hundred and twenty-five thousand?"   "No, a hundred and twenty-five people."   He could n't quite grasp that.   And yet Buffalo, South Dakota, is the largest town in a county sixty miles long by fifty wide; and of the other three towns, only one approaches it in magnitude.   Any old-fashioned family would have a greater population than either of the two remaining towns.

One day last fall I procured a substitute herder and made a quick trip to Bellefourche, just north of the Hills.   Our return journey was begun about dusk.   The roads across the gumbo belt, which is forty miles wide, are always at this season of the year as smooth as pavement. Until we reached the edge of the gumbo, houses were not infrequent, but from then on it was as if we were a comet rushing through a desolate void.   The great car took the hills like a frightened rabbit, crashed across bridges, and hurtled over the flats, forever chasing the spot of light that fled before it.   Once in a while a pin prick of light in the velvety darkness would reveal the site of some lonely ranch house or sheep wagon. Then mile after mile of blackness, with only the steady droning roar of our engine to tie us to reality. Seventy-five miles of Federal highway with never a town or a post office! The great open spaces.

Such is the land of the sheep and the herder. A great land! a free land! and, in its own way, a beautiful land. Pure, clear air; a frank, open, and friendly people; a healthful and interesting job — what more could anyone ask? Above all, the opportunity to live his own life in his own way — that is the herder's privilege and his very great reward.